WILLIAM WALLACE

WILLIAM WALLACE

THE MAN AND THE MYTH

CHRIS BROWN

Back cover image courtesy of Colin Brough.

First published 2005

The History Press
The Mill, Brimscombe Port
Stroud, Gloucestershire, GL5 2QG
www.thehistorypress.co.uk

© Chris Brown, 2005, 2007, 2014

The right of Chris Brown to be identified as the Author
of this work has been asserted in accordance with the
Copyright, Designs and Patents Act 1988.

British Library Cataloguing in Publication Data.
A catalogue record for this book is available from the British
Library.

ISBN 978 0 7509 5387 0

Typesetting and origination by The History Press
Printed in Great Britain

CONTENTS

INTRODUCTION TO THE SECOND EDITION

Since this is a revised edition I have taken the opportunity to correct a number of mistakes and make some clarification, but also to reduce the size of the volume by removing the examination and analysis of the source material which took up a great deal of space and was only of any interest to those of a scholarly inclination, which is a courteous way of saying 'total history anoraks such as myself'. All of the record and narrative material is available in printed form and should be accessible through any local authority or university library, through the inter-library loan scheme.

The purpose of this book is to provide a context for Sir William Wallace, one of the most remarkable men of medieval Europe. It concentrates on the themes that were most significant to Wallace and his contemporaries – service and allegiance. These issues were inextricably linked to status, landholding and political activity. In the environment of Scotland in the later thirteenth and early fourteenth centuries the chief focus of that activity was war, and therefore a great deal of this book is about the nature of military service, campaigning and battles. Nobody chose to make a detailed study of the Scottish military structure in Wallace's lifetime, so some of the material is drawn from the much greater – though by no means complete – data we have for the armies and practices of Robert I, but there is no reason for us to think that these were significantly different. Without the conflict brought about by Edward I, Wallace would almost certainly have never come to prominence; he would have been no more significant and no better known than any of the thousands of younger sons of obscure minor landholders who only appear very fleetingly – and most of them not at all – in the surviving records. Although there is very little information on any particular one of Wallace's contemporaries and social equals, there is a good deal of material about a large number of them scattered through narrative and record evidence; by looking at these as a whole we can get a picture of the rights and responsibilities of these men, and the issues that they had to deal with if they were to preserve themselves and their heritage through very challenging times. If this book can help the reader toward a better understanding of William Wallace and the society in which he lived it will have served its purpose.

ACKNOWLEDGEMENTS

As ever, pride of place goes to my wife Pat, who has suffered the life and times of William Wallace with a stoical grace, and to my children – Charis, Christopher, Colin and Robert – and my parents Peter and Margaret, who have also been subjected to more 'Wallace' than is fair to ask of anyone. Yet again, Robert has rescued me from self-inflicted computer disasters. Friends at St Andrews University Scottish History Department have given me a great deal of their time – Dr William Knox, Mr Alex Woolf, and others too numerous to mention – I am grateful to them all. To the staff of Easy PCs of Kennoway for their help in making the manuscript file printable, and to the late Kay Urquhart, good friend, good company and the mainstay of my babysitting in the days when I was a single parent. I am particularly indebted to Professor G.W.S. Barrow, who very kindly read the unedited manuscript of this book and made many valuable corrections and suggestions. This was my fourth book. I had expected that I would have found an effective and reliable means of blaming others for my mistakes … it is a tragedy that I have still not yet been able to do so, but hopefully I have managed to remove the majority of them now.

1

WILLIAM WALLACE, KNIGHT OF SCOTLAND

Perhaps the ultimate Scottish hero, Wallace has been dear to the hearts of Scots and others, of all ages, classes, political and religious persuasions, for seven centuries. His determination has been used to inspire soldiers, athletes and political movements. His life has inspired novelists, poets, songwriters and film-makers. A brief survey of the World Wide Web indicates a vast interest in the man, with more than one million entries for Sir William Wallace. By the same measure, it could be argued that the public interest in *Braveheart* is rather stronger, since there are more than twice as many websites dedicated to the Mel Gibson portrayal of the Guardian's political career.

Wallace has been the subject of a great many Victorian statues of questionable artistic value, several novels, at least one stage play, a film, a strip cartoon book and a number of popular, if somewhat fanciful, 'biographies'. All of these have been the work of people who have been enthused and inspired (understandably) by the life of one of the greatest, if not *the* greatest, of Scotland's heroes.

Novels, films, plays and cartoons share a common factor: nobody expects them to be strictly realistic portrayals of personalities, events or conditions – they are fantasies devised for entertainment. It could be argued, with some justice, that the latter statement also applies to the bulk of the 'biographies' of William Wallace that have appeared in recent years.

For several writers the starting point, mainstay and – in at least one example – the entirety of their primary research has been the study of Blind Harry's *The Wallace* epic. Whether the poem is a great work of fifteenth-century literature or nothing more than sheer hagiography in doggerel verse is open to debate; whether it is a generally useful record of the life and work of William Wallace is not. Harry's claim to have used an existing biography of Wallace written by his chaplain, Blair, may be true, but that does not mean that the Blair manuscript, assuming that it ever existed, bore any great resemblance either to Blind Harry's eulogy or the life of Wallace. The shortcomings of *The Wallace* as a historical record have been demonstrated many times and need no rehearsal here; what is more of an issue is the manner in which Wallace's life has been approached. Since few, if any, of the Wallace biographers have made any serious examination of the social, cultural, economic, political or military conditions of the lesser nobility in either Scotland or England in the late medieval period, they have been prone to assumptions – and perhaps a spot of wishful thinking – about the nature of the society in which William Wallace grew up and in which he made his career.

It has, for example, become an article of faith among Scots that Wallace was a man of the common people, separated from a privileged, foreign and oppressive noble class by language and social ethos. Nothing could be further from the truth. William Wallace was a product of the Scottish noble class, not an enemy of it, and not distanced from it in any cultural or political sense.[1] Like the other members of his class he grew up in Scottish communities, among Scottish people, speaking Scots,[2] but that does not have the same romantic appeal as the struggle of a man to overcome the prejudice and ineffectiveness of a class of aristocratic 'chancers', which is, broadly, the view offered in several recent biographies. The origin of the recent spate of Wallace books is, to a considerable extent, a product of the success of the *Braveheart* film – it is, as they say, 'an ill wind …' However, there has been a steady rise in interest in medieval Scotland among historians over the last forty years and much of the credit for that must go to Professors Geoffrey Barrow, Ranald Nicholson and Archibald Duncan, very much the architects of current thinking relating to Scotland in the later Middle Ages.

In 1965 Professor Barrow published the first scholarly examination of the life and reign of Robert I. Entitled *Robert the Bruce and the Community of the Realm of Scotland*, it was revolutionary in that it was a formal political biography of a Scottish king, not a collection of tales and traditions. In the same year, Professor Nicholson published *Edward III and the Scots, the Formative Years of a Military Career*, a detailed study of the final attempt of Plantagenet kings to bring Scotland directly under their sway. Both Barrow and Nicholson discovered that a great deal of light could be cast on affairs in Scotland through the study of English state records. In a sense this had been long recognised. In the late nineteenth century the Reverend Stevenson and Joseph Bain published collections of material connected with Scottish affairs. These volumes, *Documents*

Illustrative of the History of Scotland and *Calendar of Documents Relating to Scotland*, have provided medieval-ists with a wonderful resource for over 100 years. Neither Bain nor Stevenson was an analytical historian so much as an antiquarian, and Bain's lengthy introductions to each of the four volumes he compiled have not lasted the test of time so well as the body of the work. There is no such thing as a perfect work of history and both Bain and Stevenson misdated or misinterpreted the significance, or sometimes the origin, of the odd document here and there, but their scholarship and industry have been a boon to anybody and everybody with an interest in medieval Scotland.

There have, then, been two significant strands of inspira-tion driving the growth in medieval studies: the romantic – *Braveheart* and many attractive and romantic volumes from one direction; and scholarship – Barrow, Nicholson, A.A.M. Duncan, Norman MacDougall, Bruce Webster, Stephen Boardman and many more. There has been a good deal of academic research into a very wide range of social, economic and political activity in thirteenth- and fourteenth-century Scotland in recent years and a great deal of fine work has been published. Unfortunately, as any academic will be only too ready to tell, new work does not necessarily make much impact on the perceptions of the public. It is forty years since Barrow's *Robert the Bruce* was published and it is only in very recent times that his findings have started to make any impression on the kind of material that is easily available to the public.

Any book in print is, of course, easily available to the public, but generally the public will not be aware of its existence. If moved to take an interest in history, they are inclined, naturally enough, to look for information at the point of easiest access. In the past this has generally been a matter of consulting the encyclopedias or the sort of general histories of Britain that are familiar to most English and Scottish people from schooldays. 'British' histories are very frequently 'English' histories with, sometimes, a nod in the direction of Scotland, very often at Scottish heroes, including William Wallace – what we might reasonably, if a trifle uncharitably, call the 'Myth and Legend' school of learning. This has led to a historical problem in itself. In the main, English/British histories have indicated that Scotland has been essentially the same as England at any point in history, just a slightly poorer and more primitive version. This is simply not the case. There was a great deal of similarity in certain aspects of social and commercial practice in both countries, but an English traveller was just as much 'abroad' in Scotland as they would have been in France or the Netherlands.

The difficulty is that a great many Scottish people have had to 'unlearn' that sort of accidental conditioning before they can make any real headway in the study of their past. This is not an area in which there has been any great improvement in recent time. Scotland is the only country in Europe where there was, until very recently, absolutely no legal requirement for schoolchildren to be taught the history of their country. The fact that there is no adequate history textbook for Scottish schools compounds the problem, but in any case the teachers, mostly the product of Scottish education themselves, have little or no grasp of their country's history – the problem is circular. Sadly, until very recently, neither the Scottish government nor Scottish education authorities seem to have had any interest in doing anything very practical toward improving the situation, so Scottish schoolchildren have continued to be denied proper access to the history of their country.

The popular view of Scottish society in the Middle Ages has been strongly coloured by the *Braveheart* image and bolstered by many recent writers. A picture of a community that lived in mud and stone shanties, wore animal skins and conducted such trivial business as they had either by barter or by violence, under the heel of an uninterested, greedy and largely foreign aristocracy which imposed its authority with the noose. None of this is supported by evidence, but is widely accepted nonetheless. How such a crude and primitive society as twelfth-, thirteenth- and fourteenth-century Scotland managed to maintain commercial, cultural and political ties with every other country in northern Europe, build wonderful cathedrals, monasteries and castles, produce writers, scholars and soldiers of outstanding quality and survive a sixty-year series of wars of acquisition launched by a massively more powerful neighbour without effective and sophisticated administrative, judicial and above all fiscal systems does not seem to have inspired popular histories to the same degree as tales of gallantry and treachery.[3]

Fortunately, the 'Braveheart Scotland' tendency has been offset to some degree by the remarkable wave of high-quality research that has been published over the last three decades. The first two volumes of the *Edinburgh History of Scotland*, though a little dated due to archaeological and historical developments in the 1980s and 1990s, between them provide a first-class introduction to the institutions and practices of medieval Scotland. Professor Duncan's *Scotland. The Making of the Nation* explores the development of Scottish society from what we misleadingly call the 'Dark Ages' to the close of the reign of Alexander III; Professor Nicholson's *Scotland: The Later Middle Ages* takes the reader from the demise of Alexander to the death of James IV at Flodden in 1513, though it is arguable whether or not Scotland was still truly a 'medieval' society by that point. Duncan, Nicholson and Barrow were instrumental in providing a framework from which other historians could develop the various strands and themes of Scottish society. Several of these are important contributions to the theme of this book, William Wallace, not so much because they examine his life and actions, but because they examine the structures of the society in which he lived. Dr Fiona Watson's *Under the Hammer*, a study of the invasion and occupation of Edward I, is an invaluable guide to the practices of the Edwardian administration, its effectiveness, its procedures, its effect on Scottish society, and the challenges that it faced.

Any consideration of the career of William Wallace would be redundant without giving some thought to the great figures of his time, most obviously his chief adversary and eventual nemesis, Edward I. There are many biographies of Edward available, but few, if any, that compare to *Edward I* by Michael Prestwich. There is, at present, no modern scholarly biography of Alexander III which could give the reader an introduction to the society of Scotland during the youth and early manhood of William Wallace; however, there is a collection of essays ranging across economic, ecclesiastical, political and military issues in later thirteenth-century Scotland edited by Norman Reid entitled *Scotland in the Reign of Alexander III*, which cannot be too highly recommended to anyone with an interest in the life and times of William Wallace.

The political leadership of lords is an important factor in medieval history, whether in France, England, Scotland or Spain. Lordship was a rather more sophisticated relationship than we might expect and will be examined elsewhere in this book, but the interests and actions of the great magnates call for detailed study if the reader is to understand the values, benefits and problems of lord–tenant relationships. Alan Young's *The Comyns, Robert the Bruce's Rivals* and Michael Brown's *The Black Douglases* each provide an illuminating view of Scottish noble families at work. *The Comyns* shows the growth in status of a relatively minor family, who, through consistent service to the Crown and careful management of their interests, came to be one of the foremost interest groups in the country in the course of little more than 100 years. *The Black Douglases* looks at the spectacular growth of the Douglas family in the fourteenth century, in particular the meteoric rise to prominence of the 'Good Sir James', also known as 'The Black Douglas', and the means by which his personal advancement became a vehicle for the elevation of the tenuously linked Douglas families in Lanarkshire and Lothian from minor barons and lairds to membership of a vast and powerful affinity. Like the Comyns, James Douglas made his career in Crown service. Although a close associate of the king, Douglas did not join the ranks of the magnates (the greatest and most powerful and influential lords) until the death of Edward Bruce in Ireland made a gap in the Bruce party leadership that needed to be filled by a man with martial talents.

The social and economic history issues of medieval Scotland have not yet been so carefully examined by historians as the political arena, but there are useful volumes to be found, in particular Elizabeth Ewan's *Town Life in Fourteenth Century Scotland*, David Ditchburn's *Scotland and Europe* and Geoffrey Barrow's *Scotland and Its Neighbours in the Middle Ages*. Although the history of later medieval Scotland is dominated by war, there has been surprisingly little in the way of military history; though there have been a great many political histories which, for obvious reasons, can hardly avoid the topic of warfare, there has as yet been no adequate work published on the nature and practice of military service in medieval Scotland. It is not clear why this should be the case; the material is reasonably plentiful, much of it from English state records that have been available in print for 100 years and more. The absence of such a volume has led to a general perception of medieval Scottish war that almost completely fails to coincide with any of the evidence. In general terms, there was no great distinction in military dress or normal military practice between Scotland and England, or for that matter France or the Low Countries. Fortunately there have been several good studies of particular events of a military nature. There are no modern scholarly examinations of the battles of Stirling Bridge or Falkirk, but C.J. MacNamee has made an excellent survey of William Wallace's 1297 campaign in Cumbria, Westmorland and Northumberland, published in vol. 26 (1990) of *Northern History*.

Not unnaturally, Scottish historians have expended a great deal of ink on the subject of Sir William Wallace, but can hardly be expected to provide an objective view of, arguably, Scotland's greatest hero. For English historians, Wallace is a mixed bag. Many English historians, from Charles Oman (if not before) to David Starkey, have taken the view that the success of the house of Wessex in achieving dominance in southern Britain was both inevitable and desirable, and that the extension of the rule of that house, or at least its successors, to a place of superiority throughout the whole of Britain was therefore, to use a technical term from Sellar and Yeatman's masterly survey of 'memorable' English history, *1066 and All That*, a 'good thing'. From that perspective, Wallace, like Robert I, Prince Llewellyn or Owen Glendower, inevitably represented an obstacle to their preferred optimum outcome – the British Isles united in one (English) kingdom under one (English) king. The chief problem with achieving a unitary English state in medieval Britain before Edward I's reign was that no one felt particularly strongly about it; the problem after 1296 was that interest among the English generally was not so well-developed or so consistent as it was among English kings.

At various junctures, generally under threat of military force, Scottish kings had accepted the suzerainty of English ones, though the exact extent of that suzerainty was never clearly defined – an indication, perhaps, that the *realpolitik* relationship between Scottish and English kings was that both parties were involved in face-saving exercises. The Scottish kings may have resented the implications of homage to English kings, but the demands made, when they were made at all, seem to have been gestural rather than practical, indicating that English kings were unsure of their capacity to conquer Scottish kings, but that Scottish kings doubted their capacity to successfully confront their English counterparts.

Although the obligations of Scottish kings may have been nominal, they felt strongly enough about it to fork out 10,000 merks to Richard I in 1189[4] in exchange for a full discharge from all and any obligations due from Scottish to English kingship. There would seem to have been no resistance to this measure in the political community of England – no sense that Richard was selling off the assets of English kingship, no sense of national pride injured. The inevitability and desirability of a unitary English kingdom stretching from the Channel to the North Sea does not seem to have strongly motivated English political society at the close of the twelfth century. By the close of the thirteenth century the unification of Britain had become, arguably, the most significant political issue in both England and Scotland. This matter was driven chiefly, if not entirely, by Edward I's personal ambition. If it were at all possible, he intended to make Britain one kingdom under his kingship. If we assume that his goal was laudable, then William Wallace must surely be seen as little more than a political vandal.

Remarkably, Wallace has not, to any great extent, been the target for opprobrium from Unionist or English nationalist historians, perhaps on account of his outstanding heroic reputation. Like Robert E. Lee or Erwin Rommel, for some historians his reputation has stood higher than his cause. This was not the case in his own lifetime. The popularity of Mel Gibson's character from *Braveheart* among the cinema-going English of the late twentieth century was not a reflection of the popularity of the prototype among his counterparts at the close of the thirteenth century. Wallace was, to medieval English observers, a barrier to the settlement of the 'Scottish problem'. As such, it is hardly surprising that English chronicles and state records describe him as a ruthless revolutionary. Of course, one person's terrorist or gangster is another person's freedom fighter or partisan; the distinction is very much in the eye of the beholder.

It is only fair to bear in mind that there was not exactly a 'Scottish problem' in the first place. If one great barrier to British unification through English expansionism in the twelfth and thirteenth centuries was disinterest in the project among the English, the great barrier to unification after 1296 was the determination of enough Scots, enough of the time, that there should be no unification at all. In the late thirteenth and fourteenth centuries, the chief obstruction to that unification was the attitude of the Scots to what they saw as subjugation by a larger, wealthier, more populous neighbour. The importance of William Wallace to that cause cannot be questioned. His significance lies not only in his military and political successes of 1297–98, but in his commitment to his chosen cause over the next seven years. Although he never recovered the power and influence he lost after the Battle of Falkirk, his adherence to the Balliol party and the political independence of his nation never wavered. Unlike several more prominent figures, Robert Bruce among others, Wallace was absolutely steadfast in his allegiance and, like his colleague Andrew Murray, he has enjoyed a certain reputation for constancy that is shared by only a very small segment of the Scottish noble classes during the Wars of Independence.

2

OF NOBLE KIN: THE SOCIETY OF WILLIAM WALLACE

Over the centuries, Scots and others have developed a picture of William Wallace as a man of the people – not perhaps quite a farm worker, but certainly one of the 'common people' of thirteenth-century Scotland rather than one of the lords. In fact, Wallace was a member of the nobility, minor and obscure nobility perhaps, but nobility nonetheless. This is a matter of considerable importance in any assessment of Wallace's career and his impact on the political sensibilities of the Scots, both in the medieval period and, to a remarkable degree, thereafter as well.[1]

The society of thirteenth-century Scotland in which Wallace grew up was essentially a feudal one – it was not identical to that of England or France, but it bore many resemblances to both. The word feudal conjures up that familiar, if misleading, schoolbook illustration image of a pyramidal structure of society. The king sits at the top; below him is a small group of major lords; below them lesser lords; then knights; then squires; then farm tenants and finally serfs. Although such a depiction of medieval society makes for a very nice illustration, it does little to actually show the nature of rank and status relationships in medieval societies, and it is worth giving some thought to the realities of feudal society in Scotland to achieve a better understanding of the community in which Wallace lived and made his career. The king was certainly the top bough of the feudal tree, and to a great extent kings did depend on the support of the great lords or magnates, or at least on their acceptance of or acquiescence in his rule. The magnate class included the earls and the bishops, clearly denoted by their titles as superior members of the community, but it also included some great barons and heads of religious houses who did not, in any legal sense, enjoy a greater status than other barons or prelates, but whose wealth, influence or extent of property brought them into the magnate group (or they were the heads of families that enjoyed traditional status in a particular locality). In a sense, each of these men had a personal relationship with the Crown. Most of the temporal magnates held their property from the king in exchange for a variety of judicial and administrative obligations and for military service.[2]

For great lords like the Comyns or the Bruces, military service obligations were not particularly heavy, given the extent of their properties. Even for an earldom the service owed seldom exceeded ten knights, and it is believed that the customary duration of service was generally – perhaps almost universally – a period of forty days. It is clear that the 'knights' in such arrangements were frequently – in fact generally – not men who actually bore that title. In operational terms there was no real difference between knights and men-at-arms, save that a knight might be expected to fulfill a command function and that the title carried an extra shilling a day in wages. Each was obliged to equip himself to the same given standard. A man might make a lengthy career as a man-at-arms and never aspire to becoming a knight, and the fact that a property was held for the service of one knight did not mean that the tenant either was a knight himself or that he would employ a dubbed knight to discharge his obligation. Apart from anything else, there would be an obvious difficulty if the landholder happened to be a woman – the service owed for the property would still have to be provided, though there would be no question of a female landholder ever being knighted.[3]

Self-evidently, no landholder could discharge a burden of ten knights personally. Service of forty days for each 'unit' of knight service owed would come to 400 days a year out of 365. The chief means of providing for knight service was subinfeudation. A person holding land from the king might in turn grant land to a relation or associate in exchange for military service. The need for landholders to provide property or cash settlements for their children led to a degree of fragmentation of both properties and service obligations, to the extent that there are instances of landholding for fractions of knight service, generally a half or a quarter, but sometimes as little as a twentieth of a knight's service.[4] Quite how such fractions of service were discharged is unclear. Major portions of service, such as a half, could have been given on a pro rata basis, the service of twenty days rather than forty, but the service of a twentieth of a knight would only provide a man-at-arms for two days, an enlistment of limited value. There is some evidence to suggest that there was an accepted relationship between the service of men-at-arms and of other troops, specifically archers and the lighter-armed cavalry troopers known in Ireland and England as 'hobelars', allowing the substitution of lighter troops for men-at-arms. It is clear that there were alternative mechanisms which were acceptable to, or at least accepted by, both superiors and vassals, which allowed the discharge of military service obligations by a greater variety of methods than simply personal service in the field or at the castle.

Military responsibility was not limited to the individual arrangements between superior and vassal. All men were obliged to serve in the army as required in defence of the realm. Tenure for military service was an additional burden, one that depended, at least in theory, on the financial capacity to bear it; only men with a substantial income could afford the necessary investment. An act of Robert I in 1318[5] is the earliest extant statement of the extent of military responsibility for Scots, but it should not be assumed that army service was not defined from an earlier date, by custom if not through legislation. The 1318 act was primarily concerned with the arming standards of men whose landed status was not sufficient to draw them into tenure agreements. The burden was not a particularly heavy one. The poorest men in the kingdom were obliged to provide themselves with no more than a spear or a bow and some arrows. The role of such men would largely be limited to responses to invasion.

The bulk of the large armies raised by the Scots throughout the Wars of Independence would be drawn from wealthier classes of men. Those with rents worth £10 or goods worth £40 per annum were expected to equip themselves with a spear, an aketon (a padded jacket), a 'good iron' and armoured gloves. A 'good iron' was probably a steel cap. Men equipped to this sort of standard were in fact typical of the infantry element of all European armies. The chief difference between a Scottish soldier and his counterpart from elsewhere lay in his language and cultural background, not in his appearance. Although such men were recruited by the thousand when required, large field armies were something of a rarity. Wallace and Murray raised considerable forces for Stirling Bridge and the force that Wallace led at Falkirk seems to have been a strong one, but as a general rule the Scots tended to avoid major formal confrontations.

As a younger son from a modest estate, William Wallace might conceivably have served in the infantry had he not made a career of military leadership. However, his social status would more likely have led him to serve as a man-at-arms. Although the rank and file of major armies consisted of close combat infantry, the majority of warfare, in Scotland as elsewhere, was conducted by heavy cavalry. The reasons for this are wide-ranging. Partly it was a matter of economics. Although men-at-arms were expensive to train and support, even a modest force of them, particularly one with possession of the local castles, could dominate a relatively large area and provide a reasonably imposing presence in the community.[6] Being mounted, men-at-arms could respond to situations quickly, whether to intervene or to escape a larger force, but the social factors are perhaps the most significant. The men who were wealthy enough to support themselves as men-at-arms were also the men whose lifestyle afforded them the time and opportunity to learn and maintain the relevant skills. Further, since these men provided a focus of political administration and there-fore of allegiance in their localities they were, in a sense, representative of the will of the community.

No doubt Scotland, like any other country, experienced a degree of class resentment before the Wars of Independence, though there is little, if any, evidence to indicate it, but it does not seem to have been a feature of politics *during* the war, which would surely have been an excellent opportunity for the disadvantaged classes to further their position. This may in fact have occurred to some extent in a gradual and piecemeal fashion. Before the Wars of Independence most Scots were 'attached' to the land. They might have tenure rights on that land, but they themselves were owned by the landholder.

The terms most commonly used to describe these people – *rustici, nativi, bondi* and *servi* – all indicate a degree of servile status. The terms may have held a distinction that is lost to us, but they were all, in the loosest sense, serfs. By the middle of the fourteenth century serfdom would seem to have disappeared as a condition in Scotland. Throughout Europe servile status was in something of a decline, but not to the degree apparent in Scotland. To what extent the change can be attributed to the war is impossible to say, but it would seem unreasonable to think that the war was not a factor. Professor Nicholson has suggested that the rapid recruitment of Wallace's army in 1297 was fuelled by widespread social discontent;[7] however, it is not clear what evidence there is to support that observation. There is little or no trace of class resentment tending toward violence in later thirteenth-century Scotland, nor were there any events to compare with the Peasants Revolt in England or the Jacquerie disturbances in France in the fourteenth century. This does not mean that medieval Scotland was free from class conflict, or that the Scots of the day all existed in a companionable consensus, but it does suggest that class envies and insecurities were not of sufficient moment to bring about any event of great significance.

To some extent, the war itself was probably a factor in reducing the potential for social unrest within Scottish society, as opposed to unrest between interest groups. From the opening of hostilities in 1296 until the release of David II there was only a very short period, August 1305 to February 1306, when there was no party active in the cause of either King John or Robert I. The demands of the war required co-operation against a common enemy if the Scots were to succeed where the Welsh and Irish had failed in resisting the encroachment of English kings. On a more personal level, the war also made opportunities for advancement. The rate of attrition among the minor nobility was painfully high, but such men needed to be replaced if they were lost or if they were forfeited.

Several minor nobles made spectacular careers in the service of Balliol, Plantagenet and Bruce kings; we should not doubt that more obscure men improved their fortunes in the same way. Gilbert Harper,[8] a man of very obscure origins, served Edward Bruce as a man-at-arms in Ireland. Although he was considered to be of too low a station to be made a knight, he could afford the very finest in arms and armour and the men who found his body apparently thought that they had recovered the corpse of Edward himself. It would seem unlikely that Gilbert Harper's adoption of the military and (to a great, though not unlimited, extent) cultural status of a man-at-arms was the product of service in war.

There was almost certainly some degree of resentment of the Plantagenet government, by virtue of its foreign nature, if nothing else. Although there is little evidence to suggest that Edward I's government imposed heavier taxation or demanded service of any kind beyond the customary limits, there must clearly have been some issues at work to persuade thousands of Scots to risk their necks in war against an obviously powerful enemy. It is possible that the Scots thought it

likely that the occupation would lead to higher taxes, perhaps even to compulsory military service abroad. Possibly
the garrisons and administrators Edward put in place were
heavy-handed – Edward himself seems to have thought this
was a possibility, since he issued a writ declaring that in
future his officials would be more accommodating.

A motivational factor that is sometimes belittled and
often ignored in medieval history is nationalism. A number
of twentieth-century historians have seen European nationalism as a product of the wars of Napoleon, arguing that
prior to the nineteenth century the bulk of the populace in
most countries were not concerned about national identity.
In England and Scotland, at least, this is simply untenable. Thirteenth-century Scots were perfectly well aware
of their nationality, as were their counterparts in England.
The extent to which nationalism formed a vehicle for the
careers of William Wallace and Robert Bruce and the extent
to which they constituted vehicles for nationalism is a moot
point. Scots who accepted the rule of either may have done
so not out of a fondness for the Balliol or Bruce cause, but
because they believed that those parties represented the most
effective opposition to the English.

This does not mean that the non-noble classes of
Scotland were united in opposition to Plantagenet government. A group of tenant farmers on royal estates
('King's husbandmen') approached Edward I in the hope
of securing the same tenurial rights as their counterparts
in England.[9] Apart from demonstrating the willingness of
Scots of all classes to accept Edwardian rule when it took
their fancy to do so, their action shows that even Scots of
a very obscure status could be aware of themselves as a
political entity, could compare their conditions with their
counterparts in another country, and were prepared to

approach the king to seek an improvement in their status. At all levels of society, the extent to which the communities of Scotland accepted Edwardian government varied according to the prevailing political and military situation. No doubt a very large proportion of the population would have been more than happy to be simply left in peace – a common, and rational, reaction to war on one's doorstep. Even so, on the occasions that Scottish leaders called for widespread military service they do not seem to have toiled for recruits. In the weeks before Bannockburn, when, admittedly, Scotland had been at war for most of the preceding twenty years and had presumably become a rather militarised society, Robert I could afford to turn men away because they were inadequately equipped.[10]

The great formations of spearmen that are considered characteristic of Scottish medieval armies were not the means by which war as a whole was conducted; the normal practice of war was the business of men of some substance – the free tenants, the gentry and nobility. Regardless of the source of landholding privileges, whether from the Crown or from a feudal superior, in theory free tenants enjoyed heritable tenure as long as they fulfilled their contractual obligations. In practice, they naturally had to maintain a good relationship with their superior. The incidence of 'in capite' tenancies (that is to say, tenancies 'in chief' – land which was held directly from the Crown rather than from another noble) varied considerably across the country. In Lothian, the political community largely comprised free tenants of the Crown. In areas dominated by a regional magnate (such as the lords of Badenoch or the earls of Buchan in the north-east, or the earls of Carrick in the south-west) a greater proportion of the political community were vassals of magnates.

The implications for local political leadership are fairly obvious. Men and women whose place in society stemmed from their relationship with a local potentate would be inclined to be sympathetic to the interests of that person. As feudal dependants of the Stewarts, the Wallace family would have been obliged to give military, judicial and administrative service, and, to a great extent, whatever other support they could offer, politically and socially. In general terms baronial free tenants enjoyed much the same status as royal ones, but the nature of the Wallace family tenure at Elderslie may explain their absence from the Ragman Roll – it is possible that as baronial free tenants their homage was 'taken as read' by virtue of their superior's undertaking, whereas men and women of similar, or lesser, status in society were obliged to make a personal declaration of homage and fealty because they were 'in capite' Crown tenants. If that were the case, Malcolm Wallace (brother of William and the holder of the property) would not have needed to avoid appending his seal to roll; he would not have been asked to do so in the first place. This does not imply that the Wallaces were not a part of the local political community, only that their political status was, in the view of the occupation government at least, defined by their relationship with their feudal superiors.

The validity of the assumption of political loyalty on the basis of feudal obligation was, however, open to question. The presence of feudal inferiors in the ranks of Scottish armies opposed to their superiors in the ranks of English ones drew comment from chroniclers, and an English spy reporting to Sir Robert Hastang (Edward I's sheriff of Roxburgh) in 1299 described Malcolm Wallace as a member of the Earl of Carrick's following. The earl was of course Robert Bruce, but Malcolm Wallace was a vassal of the Stewart, so practical operational leadership would seem to have been rather more sophisticated than a simple matter of tenure connections.

Accepting 'feudal' as an appropriate term for Scottish structures of government in the late Middle Ages is not the same as assuming that the whole country, or even the entirety of any region within the country, was comprised entirely of feudal landholding units, nor that terms or practices were universal within those land units that were feudal. In England, the conquest of 1066 allowed William the Conqueror to apportion property as he saw fit. Land divisions seem to have remained largely unchanged at the practical level of farms and estates, but William and his successors were able to impose some degree of common practice in relation to property rights and land-holder responsibilities.

In Scotland the situation was rather more complicated – feudal tenures were introduced piecemeal, each grant made on its own terms. A number of Crown properties were converted to military tenures and no doubt other existing tenures were converted to a feudal arrangement with or without the consent of the landholders in question, but others continued to operate on the basis of property rights that had been established long before the arrival of knight service. The great English medievalist Maurice Powicke was of the opinion that there was 'no articulated system of knight service in Scotland'.[11] Writing twenty years later, Professor Barrow was equally sure that there *was*.[12] Neither chose to elaborate on exactly what they meant by an 'articulated system' of service.

In France, England or Scotland, knight service was a personal contract to provide heavy cavalry service for a specified period of time and with a specified level of equipment.

The quality of horse and arms changed over the years to reflect husbandry and technology developments, but the amount of service in terms of numbers was only very rarely altered. That amount bore no real relationship to the value or acreage of the lands for which service was due. One landholder might have 2,000 acres for the service of one tenth of a knight, while their neighbour with an estate of similar size and value was obliged to provide the service of a whole knight. In that sense, no European country had an 'articulated' system of knight service, though in Scotland it was probably an even more ramshackle affair than in France or England, due to the higher incidence of tenures that were not 'feudal' in any sense.

Sir Malcolm Wallace's status as a 'vassal' of the Stewart was hardly servile and certainly not dishonourable. Even kings gave their homage and fealty to other kings for the sake of retaining property in another country, or even in some cases for their own kingdom. The obligations attached to his landholding were of an 'honourable' nature. In peacetime a considerable portion of the tenants' obligations lay in 'suit of court'. Crown tenants, and perhaps baronial tenants as well, served as jurors in the sheriff court.[13] Baronial tenants also served as jurors in the court of the baron or earl from who they held land. Although criminal cases undoubtedly formed a significant part of the workloads of the courts, there was a great deal of other judicial activity.

It is worth examining one particular aspect of juror activity outside the criminal law in some detail. In the event of a free tenant dying, the Crown would issue instructions to the sheriffs of those counties where the deceased held land to ascertain the extent of the property, rights due to the Crown from the property and both the legitimacy and, to some degree, the suitability of the heir – the latter being largely confined to questions of the sanity of the heir, not his skills as a landholder. These enquiries are known as Post Mortem Inquisitions and where they have survived they give some insight to various aspects of landholding, as well as the work of jurors.

In 1296 the occupation government selected a number of Lothian men to conduct an inquisition into the estates of the late Robert de Pinkneye,[14] an Englishman who had inherited Luffness Castle and property around Balnacref (Balincreiff) in the constabulary of Haddington (a constabulary was a division of a sheriffdom; the sheriffdom of Edinburgh was divided into three parts, Edinburgh itself and the two subordinate constabularies of Haddington and Linlithgow). The first point of interest is that the jurors were all Scots. Edward had no intention of making major or immediate sweeping changes to the fabric of Scottish society; the only tier of government that he wanted to alter was the top one, kingship. If he could persuade the Scots that there were no radical alterations proposed for the political community at large, he might be able to bring Scotland under his rule without too much difficulty. In any case, in the short term at least, he could not allow the general conduct of commercial and social life to grind to a halt – that would hardly be a demonstration of 'good lordship'.

Without the active participation of the minor nobility in administrative spheres, Edward's government would hardly be able to function at all. If the 'business' of Scotland was not carried on under Edward's kingship, what was the point of conquest? Edward wanted an asset, not a liability. For the nobility there was really very little choice. In those parts of Scotland where Edward could effectively exert his will, the failure of free tenants to discharge their obligations was likely to lead to forfeiture, possibly even execution. The men concerned (and it would invariably have been men) might well be loath to avoid jury service. Refusal might well have implications for their own standing within the community; also, war or no war, life must go on – why should the heir to a property be denied possession of his rightful inheritance merely because there had been a war?

The deliberations of the jury probably did not take very long. They had to establish the extent of the property, its commercial value to the heir, such portions of the property as were held by others and on what basis, and the extent of military and other service due to the Crown. Where necessary, the jurors might have to conduct a survey, called a 'perambulation', to ascertain the exact bounds of the property. This was not the case in the de Pinkneye inquisition, possibly because the jurors, all local men, were sufficiently aware of what those bounds were, or possibly because there were no boundary disputes with the neighbouring landholders. The report of the jury opens with a description of the property, finding that the late Robert de Pinkneye had held the 'tenement of Balincref, and the chief messuage, with garden and pigeon house in the enclosure', worth 34s 4d per annum.

What exactly these terms imply is not always precisely clear. Evidently Balincref or 'Balnacref' – medieval spellings tend toward diversity rather than consistency – was a distinct vicinity whose limits were locally understood, and the chief house of the property had a garden, which we should probably take to mean something more along the lines of a market garden, or even allotment (though on a rather grand scale), to supply the household with the vegetables and fruit that we know were consumed in Scotland, though not grown as field crops such as kale, onions or raspberries. The pigeon house remained a feature of Scottish life until relatively recent times. Raised in pur-pose-built towers known as 'doo cots' (dovecotes), pigeons provided a source of fresh meat in winter for the tables of the gentry, and no doubt for others when the gentry were not looking – a reasonable reaction if you had a colony of rapacious pigeons in the vicinity of your crops.

Additionally, Robert had ten carucates (approximately 100 acres each) and 50 acres of arable land held 'in demesne'. This was relatively unusual in a Scottish con-text, where the tradition of the landholding classes was to rent land out for a fee (*firma*, hence 'farmer') rather than to manage it personally. In this context however, 'in demesne' may mean that the land in question was the proportion of the property he retained to provide his income, as opposed to portions of the property that he had granted to others. Each of these acres was valued at 21*d* per annum 'with its meadow and grazing'. Throughout the medieval period it was quite common to assess only the arable acreage of a property, but it was generally assumed that there would be a quantity of grazing land attached to the arable, not physically, but as a unit of land tenure. The property also had two mills, valued at £8, from which £1 per annum was given to the clerics of the hospital of St Cuthbert in alms from Robert de Pinkneye, in addition to nine bovates and nine acres which they had received from Robert and his predecessors over the years.

A number of cottars had smallholdings on the estate and paid fixed rents amounting to £5 12*s* 6*d*, and there were a number of breweries paying fixed rents of £1 9*s* 4*d*, from which Alicia de Graham was paid 13*s* 4*d* (one merk) as part of her terce from her late husband, Roger de Lelman.

The connection between Lelman and Pinkneye is unclear, but evidently Alicia's claim on the estate was not in dispute. Alicia's terce is an example of the wide range of demands that might fall upon a landholder; the sum was not large in terms of the Pinkneye estate, but it might be only one of many such obligations to family connections. Robert's brother, Henry, also had a commercial interest in the estate – six bovates which he held from his brother. Although the land was valued at £4 per annum, Henry actually paid 1*d*. Obviously that minute rental was a reflection of the relationship between Henry and Robert, not a reflection of the commercial value of the bovates. Henry's tenure was probably limited to his own lifetime; he would have to make provision for his children's future himself. If nothing else, the successor to Robert might, in due course, have to make provision for his own younger brother. Henry was not the only major secular tenant on the estate. The castle of Luffness, the demesnes of the castle and three carucates of land were rented out to Roger de Bigerton for the sum of £26 13*s* 4*d*.

At first glance this might appear to be a more carefully assessed sum, a figure of some nicety that reflects the commercial value of land in East Lothian in the late thirteenth century. However, the sum is deceptive. At two-thirds of a pound to the merk, it is clear that the rental paid was forty merks per annum. This *might* have been based on a commercial valuation but is likely to have been very favourable to the tenant. What appears to us as a favourable rental need not have appeared so at the time. It is quite possible, even likely, that some apparently favourable rentals were in fact the consequence of money lending, or at least of capitalisation of assets in some form. Many apparently generous donations of land to religious houses were in fact accompanied by a substantial cash payment to the 'donor' from the recipient of the land. It would be unreasonable to assume that activity of that nature was limited to ecclesiastical investors. It might seem curious that Robert should have let out his castle at Luffness; however, it should be borne in mind that he was the owner of the estate, not necessarily a resident. Without residents, the castle would either be a pointless financial burden on Robert or it would fall into disrepair. Roger held a further property from Robert de Pinkneye. It consisted of 'twenty merks' of land at Bynyn (Binnin) in the 'county' (constabulary) of Linlithgow. The jurors have not chosen to explain, or perhaps had no need to explain, precisely what they meant by 'twenty merks' of land. The terms 'marcate' was used fairly extensively in both England and Scotland. There is a clear link with the word 'merk' (or 'mark' in England) but it is not clear what the relationship was. The most likely possibilities are that, at some point in the past, a 'marcate' had either been worth one merk per annum in produce, or as a rental unit; the latter would suggest that the produce expected from a marcate would be worth much more than one merk, to allow the tenant to generate a profit. Alternatively, the term may have had less 'site-specific' application, but was understood to indicate an order of magnitude rather than a land unit of exactly that value.

Grants that involve the terms 'marcate' or 'librate' often represent an intention to provide land, often in a particular sheriffdom, as opposed to specific named estates. When Edward III granted several properties in the sheriffdom of Edinburgh to Sir John de Strivelin in 1335–36, he did not indicate which properties in the sheriffdom were to be given to Sir John. At that juncture Edward III happened to have a good deal of property in Lothian that he could grant out, due to the fact that he had recently forfeited 100 or so Lothian landholders for supporting the Bruce monarchy. In such circumstances, someone must have conducted a survey to ascertain which properties were available and what combination of them would constitute 100 or 200 marcates. In the absence of any evidence to indicate otherwise, it would seem most likely that administrative work of that nature would have been undertaken by jurors owing suit to the sheriff court. Those jurors would not only have a good knowledge of the local properties, they would have an understanding of the practices involved in effecting a change of lordship; also, since they would have been representatives of the local political community, their verdicts and reports might help to enhance the credibility of the administration that Edward had imposed.

There were two other sitting tenants on the Balnacref estate: Alexander de Lindsay, who held one carucate, valued at £4 per annum, for a rental of 1*d*, and Thomas de Coleville, tenant of Gosford, an area within the estate. Gosford was estimated by the jurors to extend to three carucates and to be worth £10 per annum. Thomas did not pay a cash rental at all, but instead was obliged to provide one quarter of a knight's service. How that service was expressed is not made clear, but that is probably because there was no need to do so; everyone concerned – the tenant, the landholder, the jurors and the sheriff – were all perfectly well aware of what exactly 'one quarter of the service of a knight' entailed.

For all the lands at Balnacref and Luffness, Robert de Pinkneye had owed the service of one knight – presumed to be a period of forty days – and for his property at Bynyn, Linlithgow, he owed the service of three-quarters of a knight. Self-evidently he could not discharge both obligations at the same time. In part, his problem was solved by subinfeudation. Thomas de Colville was obliged, as we have seen, to give one quarter of a knight's service. We might reasonably look to Robert's brother, Henry, who held £4 worth of property for 1*d* per annum, to be a likely candidate to discharge the balance, given his favourable rental, but if that was the extent of his wealth he might have been pushed to provide himself with the quality of equipment required for knight service. On the other hand, Thomas de Colville evidently could either provide himself with the necessary arms and horse or could afford to pay someone else to perform the service of one quarter of a knight on his behalf.

It would be unrealistic to consider Balnacref as a 'typical' Scottish property – what, after all, would constitute a 'typical' business today? All the same, the Balnacref inquisition does illustrate a number of the issues that 'typically' might apply to any property in Scotland. Estates, baronies and lordships might look like single entities held by an individual, but in practice were more often than not a patchwork of short-term, long-term, lifetime and heritable leases.

Like many other landholders, Robert's position as a rentier landlord was derived from his personal liability to provide the king with armoured cavalry service. The amount of military service required obviously varied considerably from one property to the next, but in addition to what we might call the 'field service' burden of knight service, the free tenant would also have to make a contribution, known as 'castle guard', to the security of his superior's home. Though no doubt castle guard was originally envisaged as an obligation to serve in person for a given period, it would seem that from the early twelfth century, if not before, it was acceptable – even customary – to commute such service for money payments. There are a number of reasons why commutation should have been attractive to both tenant and superior. In peacetime, the castle guards were likely to be redundant – a drain on the superior, who presumably would have to provide board and lodgings. In wartime, the addition of a couple of men-at-arms to the complement of even a very small castle was unlikely to make any real difference to its security. For the tenants, commutation was bound to be more convenient than standing guard over someone else's property.

At the time at which the original grants had been made, mostly in the early twelfth century, castle guard payments probably represented a worthwhile contribution to the security of those royal and baronial castles that attracted it, but since the payments were fixed in perpetuity, the process of inflation gradually eroded their value. By the close of the fifteenth century, castle guard payments had dwindled into an almost insignificant source of income for feudal superiors, hardly enough to make a dent in the costs of maintaining even the most insignificant of castles, let alone a garrison.

The military obligations of the nobility and the more prominent burgesses and tenants were not strictly limited to knight service; indeed, so few of the men who owed that service were actually knights that we might more realistically refer to it 'man-at-arms' service. There is a slight possibility, however, that the distinction between knights and men-at-arms was one of the methods by which fractional knight service was assessed. It was a generally established rule of thumb in France and England, and therefore very likely elsewhere as well, that a knight was entitled to double the pay of a man-at-arms. There was no real difference in the nature of their service, so far as we can tell; it was the superior social status of the knight over his undubbed companion that brought him two shillings a day instead of one. If that relationship was carried into other areas of military responsibility, it may have been the case that the service of a man-at-arms for forty days was acceptable as the equivalent of half a knight's service for twenty days, or that the quarter of a knight's service owed by Thomas de Colville on behalf of Roger de Pinkneye might actually take the form of ten days' service from a man-at-arms.

Professor Duncan has suggested that there was an accepted rate for the substitution of archers for knight service; however, while there are several extant charters that specify archer service, there are none at all that specify the service of a man-at-arms as opposed to that of a knight, though there are references to 'armed men' (*armati*) to serve alongside archers, presumably in a junior leader role.[15] This is curious, given that the bulk of the day-on-day warfare that lasted intermittently from 1296 to the middle of the fourteenth century was conducted by men-at-arms. English and Scottish chronicles and records are largely devoted to the activities of the noble class at war, because the majority of the action was conducted by men-at-arms and most men-at-arms were of the nobility.

Military service obligation for land was additional to the service owed by all the adult males of Scotland. Known as 'Scottish' or 'Common Army' service, this was an obligation on all men over the age of sixteen and under the age of sixty.[16] The fact of the obligation to bear arms is well understood; what is less clear is the extent of the burden. In 1318 Robert I laid down a scale of arms according to income. After the nature of medieval legislation generally, the 1318 rules are probably more in the nature of codifying existing obligations and/or restating existing legislation than evidence of a new system. All 'fencible' men (those liable for military service) were obliged to have arms and to bring them to community training days. It would be most unlikely that those men in the community who had the obligation – or had made the choice – to acquire more sophisticated arms would have abandoned their man-at-arms status to take part in these events. They may not have taken part at all; there is a sense in which medieval armies consisted of two distinct armies in co-operation, one of men-at-arms and one of infantry. However, it would be more likely, given that such men would be relatively well known and of some status in the community, that they would be encouraged to adopt junior leadership roles in training for the day when they might have to take the field as part of a large conventional army, such as those at Falkirk, Bannockburn or Myton.[17]

These training days were held only a few times a year, and it should not be assumed that they were all either well attended or well conducted, so the level of expertise acquired was probably not very sophisticated; however, the evolutions required of a body of spearmen are not terribly sophisticated either, and a certain amount of familiarity with those evolutions must surely have developed in most communities over the years. The essential requirements, if a formation of spearmen were to function adequately, can be seen in the foot drill manuals of any army since the invention of manuals, but with the complication that 'cadenced marching' – that is to say, marching in step – had yet to be introduced. This might seem like a trivial consideration, but is in fact quite a major advantage in moving formed bodies of men; they move more quickly and at a more consistent rate and are less likely to trip over one another if they march in step. In particular, a formation moving in line rather than column loses its 'dressing' – its regularity – very easily even when the troops are marching in step. A formation of spearmen would need to keep very good dressing to avoid becoming disrupted and vulnerable to attack. Since these training days were local affairs, such training as did take place was limited to the local men; when called to the ranks of a large army they would have to act in co-operation with the men of other localities. To achieve any degree of cohesion, there would need to have been a good deal of authority wielded at junior leader levels if the resulting army was to consist of practical formations for the battlefield, rather than a large number of independent followings.

Common army service was not the mainstay of the day-to-day Scottish military effort in the fourteenth century, but it was an integral part of the military system as a whole, and the numbers involved were considerable. In the late sixteenth century, when the population of Scotland was, if anything, smaller than it had been in 1298, the 'common army' of the sheriffdom of Carrick amounted to well over 1,000 men.[18] An indicator of the extent to which the Plantagenet administration failed to win over the population as a whole is the fact that none of the Edwards made any attempt to raise the 'common army' of any of the Scottish counties under their control, nor, so far as we know, did Edward Balliol during his attempt to procure Scottish kingship. It was certainly under consideration by Edward I – a draft for a writ to call out the men of Stirlingshire has survived, though there is no evidence that such a writ was ever issued or promulgated. Since Edward had been able to call upon service from even the most newly conquered areas of Wales with some degree of success, it seems reasonable to assume that he had, at some point, expected that he would be able to do the same in Scotland; apparently he did not feel that he could do so with any prospect of gaining men. Were he to demand service and not achieve a credible force, his authority would be undermined. Better by far not to put it to the test – a policy apparently adopted by his son and his grandson.

As well as judicial and military duties and a general obligation to be supportive of the superior, free tenants frequently had an obligation to join their superior in the hunting field. As well as contributing to the table, hunting provided an opportunity for social intercourse and, to some extent, for the practice of field and leadership skills for the battlefield. If nothing else, there was the opportunity for the lord's dependants to sharpen or develop their equestrian abilities and to become accustomed to acting collectively on horseback over a variety of terrain.

As a younger son, William Wallace would not have been expected to inherit the family property, but we should not assume he grew up excluded from noble traditions of military or hunting service. Had he married an heiress – the ambition of younger sons generally – he would have had to discharge the obligations attached to her property. Extinction in the male line was not uncommon, so marriage to an heiress was not so unlikely a proposition as it sounds and younger sons therefore needed to have the various social, judicial, equestrian and military skills necessary for life as a free tenant.

Advantageous marriage was not the only career path for younger sons, though in an economy more than 90 per cent dependent on agriculture it was surely the most popular. The only real alternatives were the Church and commerce. The latter might still be founded on matrimony. Marriages between minor nobility and burgess families were not uncommon as a means of enhancing the prestige of the burgess family and improving the finances of the noble one. Younger sons from minor noble families could be married off to burghal families and thus introduced to commerce, in exchange for a good dowry from the bride's family.[19] Towns were reckoned, with some justification, to be unwholesome places, but they were the focus of marketing. The more significant towns, the burghs, had a formal, incorporated status, generally defined in a charter stating the rights and responsibilities of the town to its superior.

Baronial and ecclesiastical burghs were not a great rarity in medieval Scotland, but almost all of the most important burghs held charters from the Crown. The responsibilities included the supply of men for the king's army and money for his treasury. The site rent of the burgh was not generally a great sum, but the burgh authorities would also have collected the customs dues and such taxes and aids as the king might be able to extract from Parliament. The most important of these revenues was unquestionably the export duty on wool. Other goods were exported, particularly fur, hides and leather, fish, woollen and linen cloth and horses, but since they were not subject to duty the extent of the trade cannot be gauged.[20]

In exchange for these responsibilities the burghs were entitled to a monopoly of trade within stated bounds, sometimes called the 'liberties' of the burghs, and the right to self-administration. Largely, if not universally, the merchant guild of the burgh came to be the dominant force in internal politics and administration. Only a very small proportion of the inhabitants of a burgh were actually burgesses.[21] Admission to the guild was dependent on a certain level of economic status and attachment to persons already admitted. In effect, the merchant guild in most towns formed an oligarchy, interested chiefly in furthering the interests of the members of the guild rather than those of the town, though to a considerable extent these did tend to be sympathetic considerations – that which was good for the merchants tended to be good for the community as a whole. Traditionally, it has been assumed that the merchants co-operated to marginalise the suppliers of produce and goods. However, recent research indicates a more consensual relationship between producers and sellers; without some degree of consensus, it is difficult to imagine how medieval towns could have survived economically, let alone managed to thrive.

That they did thrive is beyond question. In 1153 there were, to the best of our knowledge, sixteen burghs in Scotland; at the close of the reign of William I (William the Lion) there were nearly forty, and more than fifty by 1300.[22] This may be more a matter of the survival of evidence than the foundation of burghs. Many Scottish towns date their foundation from charters. The granting of a charter is not, however, very good evidence for dating the origin of the burgh, it is only evidence of the burgh being granted certain privileges. The community might have existed for centuries without acquiring the status of a burgh. There are exceptions – it seems very likely that a number of burghs in Moray were founded as planned, enclosed settlements belonging to the king, constructed to help him bring the area more securely under royal control after revolts in the twelfth century, but most burghs would appear to have developed naturally as commercial centres due to their location on navigable rivers, natural harbours or in the vicinity of secure centres of government like Stirling Castle.

A burgh did not need to be a royal foundation, though increasingly from the twelfth century (if not before) the elevation from town to burgh required royal sanction. If the status of a royal burgh was to be worthwhile it had to have privileges reserved to the burgesses and not easily acquired by newcomers to the commercial world. Several burghs were either baronial or ecclesiastical. In both cases, the intention was to give the lord or the prelate an opportunity to take advantage of a privileged position in the market.[23] Not only would they enjoy the commercial privileges of the burgesses – the merchant guild oligarchy that administered the town, not the craftsmen and servants that lived there – but they could regulate certain aspects of it, in particular letting shop and stall space and administering the sort of minor commercial justice issues that arise in any marketplace. Such issues would generally be resolved by the payment of a fine (Latin *finis*, 'an end'), which would, naturally enough, be retained by the superior.

Unlike its baronial and ecclesiastical counterparts, the royal burgh was, theoretically, free from the influence of great nobles, since it was the property of the king leased to the burgesses. In practice, burghs could not afford to offend neighbouring magnates. Apart from their general influence in the vicinity and the possibility that they might exert armed force on the burgh if pushed, the local magnatial house would often have constituted an important source of revenue. Magnates might be rich (compared to those around them, at any rate – Scottish landholders were, in general, rather less well off than their counterparts in England and considerably worse off than their counterparts in France or the Low Countries), but where is the value of having money if you do not spend it? The household of an earl or great lord, or the kitchens of a monastery, abbey or cathedral were very likely to spend large sums on expensive imported luxury goods. Their custom would help to achieve economies of scale that could not be supported by the burgh community alone.

The most profitable area of commerce was the import trade. The range of products to be found in Scottish markets was rather larger than we might expect. Spices, particularly cumin, ginger and pepper, appear regularly in rentals, clearly indicating that these products were readily available.[24] What is not so clear is why these items should be chosen as a means of expressing rents in what was unquestionably a cash economy. The expression 'peppercorn rent' no doubt has its origins in similar arrangements, and the nominal value of the rents – generally of the order of 'one pound of cumin (or pepper or ginger or galingale) valued at $2d$' – would seem to indicate that such rentals were not genuinely commercial arrangements, though it is true that the value of a produce rent such as pepper or cumin given in a charter may reflect the value of money and goods at the time the charter was granted. The penny and twopenny rents that appear in the Edinburgh sheriff's records of 1335–36 (the first year in which rents for individual properties in Scotland are recorded in large numbers) mostly refer to rentals set 200 years previously and should not be accepted as any indication of current prices and values.

The spice industry was lucrative and dependable, but the 'big money' business was probably the wine trade. Long before the days of William Wallace, a large and sophisticated commercial structure developed to supply Scottish markets with considerable quantities of wine, financed mostly by the export of wool. The cloth factories of the Low Countries may have been supplied principally from

English sources, but the Scottish wool crop was substantial enough to support a positive balance of trade and provide Scottish kings with significant revenue from customs.

One area of commerce that is likely to have seen a considerable expansion once it became apparent that war with England was a real possibility is the arms trade. Arms and armour were certainly produced in Scotland before the Wars of Independence, but the quantities are unlikely to have been large, since the market was small and wars were a rarity and tended to be brief. Men had military obligations and needed arms to fulfill them, but through most of the thirteenth century much of the martial activity in Scotland probably consisted of chasing brigands.

In 1296, the most recent Scottish military operation had been the annexation of the Isle of Man, some twenty years previously. The Man expedition did not involve a very large force, nor was the campaign long or challenging, so the experience gained was marginal in itself, as well as being twenty years out of date. All the same, men needed arms and the Scots who were beaten at Dunbar in 1296 do not appear to have been noticeably ill-equipped, though it might well be the case that their equipment was rather old-fashioned – but then, a society unaccustomed to war was unlikely to invest a great deal in arms and armour if they were never required to do more than chase bandits.

Arms could be bought; an entry in the plea rolls of Edward I's army in Scotland in 1296[25] refers to the theft of swords from a Scottish shop. Indeed, the Scottish name 'Lorimer' means armour or harness maker, but for fashionable, state-of-the-art equipment, Scottish nobles probably had to purchase weapons and armour of foreign manufacture. Throughout the Wars of Independence, most of the imported arms came from the Low Countries or from

France, though repeated demands from English kings that Irish and English merchants should refrain from exporting arms to Scotland suggests that commercial considerations could be more important than patriotic ones.[26]

A career in the Church would generally require some sort of outlay from the family resources, either by purchasing a living in a monastery or through parish patronage rights. When a lord gave land for the construction of a church and the support of the priest, he might well retain the right of 'advowson': the power to appoint a new incumbent should the old one die or move on elsewhere. Such patronage was a saleable commodity; a position as a parish priest or other forms of benefice could be purchased from the holder of the advowson.

Military service by Scottish clergymen seems to have been something of a rarity, though not unknown – the rector of Pencaitland served in the Plantagenet garrison of Edinburgh Castle in the 1330s with a tiny retinue of two men-at-arms.[27] Those clerics who came from noble families (and that would have been the vast majority of them) would have had the same sort of education as their peers; military, judicial and hunting duties would have formed a considerable part of that education. The family property would descend to the eldest son, and it might seem redundant that his younger brothers should have the same sort of education and training, since they would not become the head of their branch of the family; however, an eldest son might die before having an heir of his own, particularly in wartime, and a younger brother would need the practical skills required of a landholder should he happen to inherit the family property.

For most people today, the concept of family property has little, if any, significance, but in medieval Scotland it was of prime importance. The family property was not merely the home and source of income of the head of the family, but the source of support for members of the family through generations. Portions of the family estate would be granted to various relatives to provide for them and their families. Should someone inherit property while their mother was still alive, a portion of the land – nominally a third and known as a terce – would usually be granted to the mother of the heir to provide her with an income for the rest of her life, after which point it would revert to the family estate.

Had William Wallace made a conventional career, he might have spent his days as a very minor member of the political community, holding a slice of his brother's estate in liferent. On his death, that slice would be restored to the main property, so Wallace would have to have made provision for his own sons or see his branch of the family decay in status.

Most agricultural land in Scotland was tenanted, even the estates of relatively trivial landholders, so Wallace might never have put his own hand to the plough, but as the dependant of a very minor landholder it would be rash to assume that he enjoyed a notably better standard of living than his more successful tenants. The preponderance of farms would seem to have been held by groups rather than individual tenants. The root of multiple tenancies probably derived from a need to collectivise labour and plant in the form of draught animals, to achieve commercially viable farms. Demesne farming, lands retained in the lord's hands and under his own (or his grieve's) management, though highly developed in England, does not seem to have been a widespread commercial practice in any part of medieval Scotland. The numerous example of farms bearing the name 'mains', a corruption of 'demesne', would seem to indicate the sort of arrangement more commonly called 'home farms' in England – a means of providing produce for consumption rather than for sale.

The Scottish nobility of the thirteenth and fourteenth centuries were essentially a class of rentier landlords with military and legal obligations and the Wallace family formed a tiny part of that class. The noble status of the Wallaces was not sufficiently exalted to give them entry to the upper reaches of political society. Although they may have been members of the same class as the earls and great lords, the Wallaces were almost as much removed from the senior aristocracy as they were from the poorest of villeins.

This would have a considerable effect on the career of Wallace. His attainment of power was achieved through successful military leadership, not through his social position. So long as that leadership continued to bring results against the occupation, Wallace could retain political leadership as well. Once he had been defeated his influence started to wane almost immediately, due to the fact that he had no customary body of support within the political community as a whole and, crucially, no network of sympathisers within the senior aristocracy. This might have been offset had Murray not died in the weeks after Stirling Bridge. Murray may not have been in the first rank of Scottish magnates, but he was well known and wealthy. The magnate class might have been rather more willing to accept the leadership of Murray, the eldest son and heir of a senior baron, rather than Wallace, the younger son of a minor laird.

3

THE ROOTS OF THE WAR

Throughout the reigns of Alexander II and Alexander III, Scotland and England had enjoyed a stable and generally peaceful relationship. Although Scottish trade continued to be chiefly with France and Flanders, commercial and cultural activity between the two countries would seem to have increased steadily through the thirteenth century.

Following the death of his son and heir, Alexander remarried in 1285. He was still only in his early forties and could be reasonably hopeful of fathering another son and living long enough to see his son grow to adulthood before inheriting the throne. On 19 March 1286, despite the entreaties of various Crown servants and officers who suggested he should wait overnight for a storm to pass, Alexander decided to make his way to his wife. Unfortunately for all concerned, he never arrived, but was found dead at the base of a cliff near Kinghorn in Fife. The queen claimed that she might be pregnant, and matters stalled for a short while before it became clear that she was not. This meant that Alexander's heir, his granddaughter

Margaret, was the heir to the throne. Margaret's mother had been queen of the late king of Norway.

Despite her tender years, Margaret's marriage had already been a matter of discussion between Alexander III and Edward I. It had apparently been broadly agreed between them that Margaret should marry Edward's son (Edward of Carnarvon, later Edward II of England), thus bringing about an eventual union between England and Scotland under the rule of Edward and Margaret's son, assuming that they had one. This proposed union does not seem to have been an unpopular plan. Scotland and England had been at peace for most of the preceding century and there was no strong tradition of antipathy between the two nations. A number of issues had to be addressed – in particular, guarantees for the traditions of Scottish law and the preservation of ecclesiastical independence for the Scottish Church – but it would seem that a dynastic union was not seen as a threat by the Scottish political community. Margaret's death en route from Norway to Scotland destroyed any possibility of that union, and the Scots were left with the thorny problem of selecting a new king. There was no shortage of candidates; on the other hand, who exactly was going to make the decision?

The council of Guardians, originally set up to rule on behalf of Margaret during her minority, has been roundly criticised by Scottish historians for approaching Edward I at all, but in fact their choice was both practical and inevitable. Edward's reputation as a 'second Justinian' is largely the product of Victorian wishful thinking, but is not wholly unjustified. He was a jurist of repute and ability, but was not above radical reinterpretations of legal practice when it suited him. Perhaps more significantly, he was the king of Scotland's only geographical neighbour; he was likely to be acceptable to all of the claimants; he had had a good relationship with Alexander III and, though Scots would deny it, he had, in his own view at least, certain 'rights' in relation to Scotland.

Edward's 'right' stemmed from a number of occasions when Scottish kings had accepted the overlordship of English kings – generally, if not invariably, as a result of military defeat. Henry III made some attempt to resurrect that type of relationship when Alexander III came to the throne, and Edward I made a similar attempt when, on his own accession to the throne of England, Alexander came to perform homage for the various properties he held in England. Like his predecessors, Alexander held extensive lands in England, just as the king of England held extensive lands in France. In each case, the homage and fealty requirements of landholding presented a problem for the superior and the inferior. For the inferior, there was the issue of whether their prestige as a king was undermined by giving homage, or to what extent, if any, their homage for lands in a foreign kingdom affected the sovereignty of their own kingdom. For the superior, homage might afford an opportunity to gain prestige by accepting homage from a king, or to 'stretch the envelope' of the homage commitment to extract a political advantage. Homage and fealty had to be renewed at the death of either party, so the issue arose fairly regularly.

After Edward I became king in 1272 he naturally wanted the homage and fealty of all of his barons, including Alexander III, who held extensive land rights in Tynedale and elsewhere. During the ceremony, Edward tried to insert a measure into the formula which would mean that Alexander would have accepted him as his superior and lord, not only for his English properties, but for his kingdom of Scotland. Alexander refused, saying that he held his kingdom from God alone, and Edward chose not to press the point, effectively accepting that he had no legal position in respect of Scottish kingship.

As far as the Scots were concerned, any rights that English kings might have enjoyed in Scotland had been extinguished by the Quitclaim of Canterbury in 1189,[1] when Richard I of England had sold any and all English Crown interests in Scotland for the sizeable sum of 10,000 merks (one merk, or mark in England, was equivalent to two-thirds of one pound – thirteen shillings and four pence), but effectively the Scots could hardly avoid asking for Edward's help; not only was he a noted jurist, he was the king of Scotland's only neighbouring country and a mighty prince. If his help was not sought, he might well impose it anyway. That help was forthcoming, but only on Edward's terms. As a precondition of participation in the contest, all of the claimants had to accept Edward's right to conduct the court and his superiority. Most of the claims were, superficially at least, relatively frivolous. Those with no expectation of outright success were looking for opportunities. If, for example, the new royal line should fail, there might be a new competition, and anyone who had failed to make their case in the first contest would be unlikely to be accepted into a second. Furthermore, those whose claims were unlikely to bear fruit directly might be able to profit from lending (or selling) their support to one or other of the more serious candidates; also, the Canmore line of the Alexanders had failed, so why not the Balliol or Bruce line? If the new Scottish king should happen to die without an heir, the whole business of the Scottish succession might have to be examined afresh. Men who had been passed over for the Scottish throne might be able to extract some concession or advantage from a second 'competition', but only if they had declared an interest at the outset.

The two most significant claimants were Robert Bruce of Annandale, a prominent lord and grandfather of the Robert Bruce who would eventually become king, and John Balliol. Each of these men was descended from the royal house, and in very similar degree. A third candidate, Sir John Hastings, claimed that the kingdom of Scotland was a fief of the English Crown and, as such, should be divided equally between himself, Bruce and Balliol, just like any other Crown fief inherited by females. Hastings's plea was rejected by Edward I on the grounds that, as a kingdom, Scotland was not a divisible inheritance. The court was conducted between 1291 and 1292. A total of 104 auditors were appointed. The selection of auditors reflected the political realities of the situation. The Balliol and Bruce camps appointed forty each, the balance being selected by Edward I. The eventual decision to appoint John Balliol has been seen, by Scottish medievalists particularly, as an indication that Edward perceived John to be a more malleable person than Robert Bruce. This may have been true, but the evidence does not indicate that Robert would have been any less amenable to Edward's influence. John, in common with all the other competitors, had accepted Edward's superiority as a condition of being accepted as a claimant at all, and was in any case already a homager of Edward for several properties in England, a distinction he shared with Robert Bruce.

Edward may have chosen John, but he was determined to make clear to him that he reigned under Edward, not independently of him.[2] Within a year or two, Edward was demonstrating his suzerainty by undermining John I's government. In medieval societies the role of the king as the final judge of appeal was very important, both as a matter of judicial practice and as a demonstration of the king's ability to exert lordship. Edward made it clear that he was willing to hear appeals against the judgements of John, just as if he was any English baron. In fact, it seems more or less certain that Edward encouraged at least one person, Roger Bartholomew, a Berwick merchant, to bring a case before Edward which had already been heard, and rejected, by John. Naturally, such behaviour undermined John's prestige and authority and led to resentment of Edwardian interference. Not content with interference in appeals procedures, Edward decided to demand military service from the king of Scotland as a vassal of the king of England. Whether Edward actually expected to gain troops by this measure is unclear, though since various Scottish lords had campaigned with Edward in France, Wales and Palestine, he may have expected the support of a few. It is more likely that he was simply trying to force John into a reaction that would allow Edward to depose him and to annex Scotland.

It is by no means certain that Edward had had that intention since the demise of Alexander III, but it can hardly be denied that he was willing to make an opportunity for intervention from the earliest days of John's kingship. John's refusal of service and his repudiation of his homage to the king of England provided Edward with, in his view, excellent grounds for war. Although his summons to the Scots for military service had failed, Edward was still able to take advantage of divisions among the Scots. There is some doubt about the stability of John's government even before his defiance of Edward. English chroniclers tell us that a council of twelve prominent men had been elected to govern the country on John's behalf. The chroniclers may have been confused about the Guardianship that existed between the death of Alexander III and the installation of John I and concluded that that council of worthies had either continued to rule, or recovered their power, during John's kingship, or there may indeed have been such a council of government. However, it is not inconceivable, though highly unlikely, that the council was simply an invention of Bruce propaganda in the fourteenth century, aimed at undermining any vestiges of respect for the Balliol dynasty. The Bruces would in fact maintain that John had never really been the legitimate king of Scotland, merely an appointee of Edward I. Charters of Robert I describe Alexander III as 'our immediate predecessor as King', thereby denying the very existence of John's kingship.[3]

John's defiance in 1295, and his commitment to a treaty with France against England, prompted Edward to mount a Scottish invasion in the spring of 1296. The Scottish nobility as a whole had accepted Edward's leadership during the 'Great Cause', and several influential men, for a variety of reasons, chose to serve Edward against John I. A number of Scottish lords probably had real doubts about what exactly was the ethically 'correct' position to adopt. John may have been their feudal superior but Edward was John's feudal superior, so which level of command should take precedence? On a purely practical level, there was the question of military competence. The Scots had not been at war for more than thirty years, and there had been very little fighting then. The English on the other hand had a well-established military system and a great deal of relatively recent military experience. Some Scots were in fact active in support of the Plantagenet cause. The Bruces adopted the Plantagenet cause through a mixture of antipathy to John Balliol, whom they resented because he had won the position that they felt was rightly theirs, and, perhaps, hope that Edward would depose John and replace him with Robert. John Balliol's army would inevitably be much weaker than Edward Plantagenet's, and the defection of the Bruces and others would weaken it even further.

Inexperienced, divided among themselves and, apparently, in the absence of their king, the Scots raised an army and mounted raids into England in support of the commitment to the French, but the amateur nature of their approach to war achieved little or nothing. Cross-border raiding was likely to make no real impression on Edward, but the claim that the Scots had set fire to a school at Hexham and burned more than 200 young scholars to death probably did his cause no harm in the propaganda battle, though it is extremely unlikely that a place like Hexham would have a school with anything like 200 students. While the Scots made ineffectual raids in Northumberland, Cumbria and Westmorland, Edward's army advanced on Berwick. Initially the town made a stout defence, but the defences of the town were not adequate to the task of keeping out a strong and well-motivated enemy. The town fell to storm and was sacked with enormous loss of life – apparently the dead were so numerous that they could not be buried and the bodies had to be thrown into the sea.

This was not the full extent of Scottish resistance to Edward's army, however. The castle of Dunbar was held against them, and there was a Scottish army mustered nearby at Caddonlea.[4] However, the two armies did not clash. At the end of April 1296 a portion of the Scottish cavalry encountered one of the four English cavalry formations and were quickly routed. It is very unlikely that the Scottish force comprised all or even necessarily a large proportion of the men-at-arms in the Scottish army.

It would have been very bad practice indeed for the entire armoured cavalry element of the army to be detached from the rest of the force without a very clear and attainable goal, and for an operation for which the chances of success were very high and the potential damage from success or failure would be negligible. Medieval armies, like modern ones, depended on the effective combination of various arms to achieve victory, so the loss of the heavy cavalry would compromise future operations and put the main body of the army at risk. The impact of a sharp reverse on the morale of the army was probably another significant factor in convincing the Scots leadership that there was no point in continuing the fight, but to do so with no mobile force under command would have been suicidal. The men-at-arms element of the army could operate, under certain conditions, without the immediate support of infantry, but the infantry would be near-helpless without the cavalry if they were confronted by a force of all arms.

Dunbar Castle was surrendered almost immediately and the English pressed on to Edinburgh. Already a well-developed fortress, Edinburgh withstood five days of bombardment before surrendering.[5] Assuming that the castle was adequately stocked with supplies and that the garrison was large enough for the task, it might be reasonable to ask why it should have surrendered so quickly; however, all of the strongholds that fell to Edward in 1296 shared a common problem. They might be able to withstand a siege for some time, weeks or even months, but without relief they must all surely fall eventually. Stirling Castle was left in the care of the gate porter, the rest of the complement having decided to return to their homes, presumably in the hope of avoiding any recriminations in the wake of Edward's victory, and because there was no realistic hope of rescue. In the aftermath of the fight at Dunbar and the subsequent disintegration of the Scottish army, where was such a relief column going to come from? A considerable portion, at least 200 men, from the class that provided the traditional source of political and military leadership had become prisoners of war in the spring and summer of 1296, and the bulk of the rest of the Scottish political community, particularly in the southern and eastern counties, had accepted Edward's lordship by the end of August that year, under the terms of the Ragman Roll and/or in personal submissions.[6]

Who, in any case, could claim the authority to demand the military service and financial contributions that would be necessary if the Balliol cause was to make a recovery? John had been deposed and was hardly in a position to appoint a Guardian to further his interests.

The Scots had, of course, been confronted with this sort of problem in the past. When Alexander III died unexpectedly in April 1286, a council of Guardians was quickly appointed to administer the country and look after the interests of the Crown. When Margaret died in the winter of 1290 there had been no clear heir to the throne, but the political community had arranged for the business of the country to proceed. However, these two situations were very different from that in 1296. On the previous occasions the country had not been at war, did not have an occupation government and army to deal with and, crucially, there was no division between those who had accepted the rule of the Plantagenets and those who had not.

Edward spent the summer of 1296 making a progress through the eastern seaboard counties as far as Elgin, accepting homages and fealties from magnates, minor nobility and burghs. Content that he had essentially dealt with the 'Scottish problem', he returned to more pressing affairs, specifically his conflict with France. His confidence that his lieutenants could be trusted to finish the job of annexation was misplaced. Within a year, Edward was being informed that, of all the counties in Scotland, only Berwick had a proper structure of administration in the Plantagenet interest.[7] Not only were the other counties outside English control, but the Scots had started to appoint sheriffs and other government officials on behalf of the Balliol cause. The source of this information was Hugh Cressingham, Edward's chief administrator in Scotland and, as such, a man likely to have a pretty clear idea of the extent and effectiveness of the Plantagenet occupation.

One of the reasons for Edward's failure to turn his defeat of the Scots into annexation probably lay in the fact that he did not fully appreciate the sheer size of the undertaking. Map-making was not yet an exact science, or even a particularly well-developed art. Edward almost certainly did not realise that he had in fact traversed only a relatively small portion of Scotland. He had been able to extract homage and fealty from a large body of the political communities of the southern counties, but had made little progress in the north and west. The Ragman Roll exercise had brought about 300 people from Lothian alone into Edward's peace, but only three from the entirety of Ross.[8]

It seems very likely that Edward had no plans to change the general administration of Scotland, only to replace John and his officers with himself and men of his own choosing. He may in fact have expected that there would be little or no reaction to this change of dynasty among the Scottish political community – why should a different head under the crown make any great difference to the lives of the subjects? Certainly his initial dispositions of troops were hardly major deployments. When he first appointed a sheriff for Edinburgh, during the succession dispute, Edward allocated ten men-at-arms to form the sheriff's retinue. This was probably in line with, if not identical to, the size of complement that had been maintained under Alexander III[9] and may indicate a policy of promoting an image of 'business as usual' in local government. However, his garrisons may have been established with a view to discouraging unrest between the Scottish political factions. Even a very tiny token force would be an indication to ambitious Scottish magnates to refrain from trying to improve their position through force – if they wanted to seize a royal castle they would have to dislodge Edward's men, an action that would provoke Edward into a reaction that was likely to be both swift and violent.

It should not be assumed that ten men-at-arms was the sum total of the force theoretically available to the sheriff of Edinburgh. Like his predecessors under King Alexander, the sheriff would have the authority to demand the customary military service of the local political community. The lairds, lords and the more prosperous burgesses of Lothian, like those of other counties, had an obligation to discharge military service as men-at-arms, for a fixed period, probably forty days. Presumably these men were 'rotated' so that a number of them were available at any given point in the year.

The most fruitful sources of material relating to military service are government records – garrison muster rolls, victualling arrangements, payrolls and the valuation of chargers. Men on active paid service in Plantagenet armies and garrisons were usually (though not, apparently, universally; see Dr Ayton's *Knights and Warhorses* for a thorough examination of cavalry service in the armies of the three Edwards) entitled to have one of their horses valued for replacement costs by Crown appointees. Men giving customary service were not paid wages, nor were they normally entitled to 'restauro' payments for lost horses – their forty days' service, with an adequate mount, was part of their land rental. Failure to provide that service could lead to forfeiture and, in the absence of extensive forfeitures among the Scottish minor nobility in 1297 we must assume that a fair quantity of the due service was in fact discharged. The men in question had little choice. In areas where King Edward's government was functioning effectively, it would be almost impossible to avoid compulsory, customary service obligations without incurring the displeasure of the government.

This does not mean that Edward did not face opposition. A considerable number of men were forfeited and then restored to their properties in 1296–98.[10] To what extent this was the product of continued activity against the Plantagenet government after Dunbar and to what extent these restorations indicate men accepting Edward's kingship in the light of defeat in the summer of 1296 is impossible to say, but clearly Edward felt that there was every chance of effecting a relatively painless annexation of Scotland, and that existing sources of leadership and influence could be persuaded to accept his authority.

In theory, at least, the Ragman Roll and other submissions should have helped to secure Edward's position in Scottish affairs. The men and women who declared their allegiance to Edward represented the class of government in its widest sense – not simply the great lords, but the class of minor landholders, lairds, who carried out a great deal of the actual business of government, particularly judicial and military activity. If they could be induced to accept Edward, and to remain in his affinity, he should have had little to fear from insurrection. Each of these men and women had bound themselves personally to Edward's cause, after all. The problem was, how reliable were these declarations? Even men who had joined Edward's army in 1296 could not always be relied on to toe the party line. Robert Bruce (the one who would become king in 1306) had committed himself to the Plantagenet cause, campaigning on Edward's behalf in 1296, but by the summer of 1297 had defected to the Scots.

Quite what moved Bruce to align himself with Andrew Murray and William Wallace against the Plantagenet cause in that year is open to question. Murray and Wallace were unreservedly committed to the Balliol kingship, whereas Bruce had unquestionably been Edward's 'man' for years. He had appended his seal to the Ragman Roll, his grandfather had accepted Edward's suzerainty over Scotland, and his father was sufficiently in favour with the English king to serve as his sheriff of Carlisle. Should a revolt against Edward lead to the restoration of King John, any ambitions the Bruce family held in relation to the Scottish crown would be stopped dead in their tracks. Worse than that, a restored John might take exception to the fact that the Bruces had refused to serve in his army in 1296, turning out for Edward instead. If the Balliol cause seemed like a hopeless venture in 1297, one must question Robert's involvement – what did he hope to achieve? Alternatively, if the Balliol cause was looking quite promising, how did he hope to reach an accommodation with King John in the light of Robert's service to King Edward?

One possibility is that Robert did not in fact consider the Balliol cause a viable proposition in itself, but believed that the English were incapable of permanently acquiring

Scotland. If that were the case, he might be well advised to ensure that he was seen as a force in the struggle against King Edward, particularly if he retained his ambition for the crown. If Scotland were to become an independent country again, he would have little influence in the post-war settlement if he had not been involved in the struggle. Conceivably, Robert may have been trying to exert political leverage on Edward I. If Edward's administration proved unequal to the task of assimilating Scotland, it might be more in his interests to install a Scottish king once more, as he had done in 1292. No doubt Robert would have been more than happy to accept kingship at Edward's hand, but he would first have to demonstrate that he was a power-ful figure in the Scottish political landscape, who would be capable of keeping his subjects under control should he gain the throne and an unequivocal allegiance to Edward I. Edward, of course, was no fool, and would have been well aware that to reconstitute Scottish kingship would be a hostage to fortune. He might be able to keep a sub-king in order, but would his descendants be able to do so?

Given that Bruce and Wallace were both at war with England in 1297, it might be reasonable to ask why Wallace did not choose to support a Bruce bid for king-ship. First and foremost, Balliol was the legitimate king whereas Bruce would be a usurper. In the diplomatic arena, John could reasonably be described as a duly constituted king who had been deprived of his realm by a neighbour. There would probably be more popular sympathy with the cause of John Balliol, a king deposed, than there would be for Robert Bruce, an earl with ambition. The Balliol name would have been better known than that of Bruce outside Scotland. As an earl, and, after the death of his father, the holder of the extensive lordship of Annandale, Bruce would have had significant financial and military resources and a position of some prominence politically, but he was only one of a dozen or more men of similar status in Scotland.

Had Wallace decided to support a Bruce bid for kingship, he would have alienated several leading magnates who preferred the 'legitimist' succession of the Balliols. In any case, a Wallace–Bruce partnership would have had to depend on the willingness of Robert to nail his colours to the mast. As long as he could claim to be acting on behalf of his liege lord, King John, Robert could retain a realistic hope of making his peace with Edward, should that become expedient. Were he to claim the throne in his own right, he would lose any prospect of an accommodation with Edward I other than by outright military victory. Even with the unquestioned support of the entire political community of Scotland, that would have been, to say the least, a daunting task. Far from being sure of that support, Robert could reasonably rely on the outright opposition of a considerable body of opinion within the 'patriotic' party, let alone from those who had accepted Edward I's kingship before the Strathord armistice. It would seem much more likely that Bruce offered to bide his time, presumably waiting for Edward I to die, before making his move. His 'bond' with Bishop Lamberton, which was made at Cambuskenneth Abbey at about the time of Edward I's siege of Stirling Castle in the spring of 1304, required him to find the sum of £10,000 – a fortune which would probably have been well beyond the resources of either party – should he undertake any 'arduous business' without consulting the bishop first.[11]

In addition, if Wallace were to endorse Robert as king he would utterly compromise his own position. Very few political figures in any period of history have willingly given up a position of great authority. Wallace's Guardianship was completely dependent on his success as a military leader, a fact clearly demonstrated by his loss of the Guardianship immediately after his defeat at Falkirk. It is reasonable to assume that he did not intend to be defeated and that he planned to carry on as the principal figure of authority in Scottish political life. Had he helped Bruce to become king, he would have had to surrender his own power immediately. This would obviously have been the case had Wallace succeeded in restoring John I to the throne. However, he could be reasonably confident that John would reward him suitably, whereas Robert might well think it desirable to marginalise Wallace in the interests of confirming his own authority, and to suppress any suggestion that his kingship was dependent on the efforts of a man from a minor lairdly family.

There is no suggestion from contemporary accounts to suggest that Wallace ever entertained the possibility of helping to erect a Bruce kingship; he seems to have been totally committed to the Balliol dynasty. Of course, while Wallace was crucial to the Balliol cause, the Balliol cause was crucial to William Wallace. Without his affiliation to, and acceptance by, the Balliol party, Wallace's actions in 1297 would have been acts of brigandage rather than of policy. In peacetime there was no real possibility of a man from Wallace's background rising to a position of national prominence – senior political leadership was very much the province of the magnate class.

Oddly, however, the relatively junior status of Wallace may conceivably have helped to make him acceptable, as a temporary measure at least, to the more senior members of the community that embraced the Balliol cause. A man of Wallace's station had no claim, however tenuous, to the throne, nor would he ever be able to develop the kind of power base that might enable him to bid for the throne by force of arms. So long as his commitment was to the Balliol kingship – a loyalty in which he never wavered so far as is known – Wallace did not represent a long-term threat to the prominence of the magnate families, though perhaps, had he been successful in effecting the restoration of King John, he might reasonably expect to have been rewarded sufficiently well to enable him to join their ranks.

In all medieval European kingdoms it was expected that service should bring rewards. A king could be given no greater service than the restoration of his kingdom. If successful, Wallace could reasonably expect to receive grants of land, money and office and/or a very advantageous marriage through the offices of a grateful monarch. The latter was obviously preferable from the point of view of the king; it cost nothing of itself, and though if the marriage was seen as 'disparaging' to the bride that would reflect badly on the king, it would have been obvious that Wallace would have to be rewarded suitably or *he* would be disparaged – still a poor reflection on the king. It is unlikely that a man who had achieved such a project would be willing to return to obscurity and life on the farm, or that anyone would expect him to, but the restoration of the king would inevitably mean the loss of Guardianship and would call for action on the part of the king to secure a position within the senior aristocracy for Sir William Wallace as compensation, as well as out of gratitude and a desire to keep Wallace firmly in the Balliol camp should King John regain his kingdom.

4

FROM GANGSTER
TO GOVERNOR

The information relating to William Wallace before his rise to military and political prominence in the summer of 1297 is scarce almost to the point of invisibility. His birth date is unknown and his birthplace unverifiable. Although Wallace has traditionally been associated with Elderslie in Renfrewshire, there is precious little in the way of evidence to substantiate the claim. James MacKay has made a case for associating William Wallace with Ellerslie, Ayrshire, a small village and colliery that disappeared in the middle of the last century.[1] Most of the early exploits of William Wallace seem to have occurred in and around Ayrshire, and there was a relatively high incidence of the Wallace surname in the sheriffdom.[2]

A good deal had been made of the absence of William and his immediate family from the Ayrshire entries of the Ragman Roll. However, two Ayrshire Wallaces, Alan (Aleyn) and Nicholas, did append their seals to the roll, thereby acknowledging the sovereignty of Edward I. Alan is one of a relatively small number of homagers described as 'king's tenants', sometimes described as Crown tenants by historians. In the strictest sense, everyone was either a tenant or subtenant of the Crown. However, most people who held property directly from the Crown did so on very easy terms indeed. The lesser nobility who appear as minor 'in capite' tenants, do so in groups described as being 'of the county of' Fife/Aberdeen/Dumfriesshire as appropriate. The 'king's tenants' are clearly differentiated from the 'county' homagers, though there was no social or economic divide between the two groups. It would seem safe to conclude that the 'king's tenant' rentals were more economically realistic than those due from 'county' homagers, but the two groups were not separate entities. Several men and women appear in both categories – often, though not always, in the same sheriffdom.

As a king's tenant, Alan Wallace would have had the same social, legal and military obligations as his neighbours, but would probably have paid a great deal more rent. However, the chief difference in their tenures was whether they were heritable. King's tenancy landholding was, therefore, more ministerial in nature and was probably the more traditional form of land tenure. These properties probably had their origins in the thanage and drengage tenures of ninth- and tenth-century (if not earlier) Lothian and Northumberland, many of which had been converted to knight service tenures in the early twelfth century to provide Scottish kings with the weapon of choice of the later medieval period, the man-at-arms.[3]

The significance of Alan Wallace may be greater than one might suppose. In the Mitchell Library in Glasgow[4] there is an imprint of both the obverse and reverse sides of the seal of William Wallace, Guardian of Scotland, apparently made in 1912 by one P. Sinclair Rae. The lettering has been identified by Professor A.A.M. Duncan as reading 'William son of Alan'. There are several possibilities – it is perhaps just conceivable that the piece is a forgery, in which case it would be reasonable to expect that the forger would have avoided anything that might lead to controversy – there would have been no need to include the name of the principal's father. It is also a theoretical possibility that the seal-carver simply made a mistake, Alan and Adam are fairly similar names, after all. However, the great importance of seals for all sorts of administrative, financial and personal business and the care required to cut the seals would surely mean that seal-makers were likely to be painstaking individuals. Even if they were not, even if the carver had made a mistake, there is no reason to assume that nobody else would have noticed – William Wallace, for example. It is of course just about possible – however improbable – that when he took delivery of his new seal as Guardian that he did not think to examine it; had he done so he would surely have noticed if his father's name was wrong and would just as surely have demanded a replacement.

Another aspect of William Wallace's seal (as Guardian: it is quite possible, even likely, that as a young man of no great social or political significance he would not have invested in a seal of his own, but would have made use of the seals of others for those odd occasions when he needed one) is of course the image of an arm holding a bow. A number of writers have taken this as evidence to support the statement of the Lanercost chronicler that Wallace had been an archer and/or leader of brigands, and that he made his living by 'the bow and quiver'. How he would have made a living as an archer in Scotland before the war is not clear. There was little if anything in the way of employment for a military archer, and hunting was the sort of thing that people did themselves for entertainment – they did not hire others to do it for them. The motifs used on seals, like heraldry, might contain a 'pun' on the name of the owner, but that would be the exception rather than the rule. Most seal emblems are quite arbitrary, as much a reflection on the imagination of the owner and the talents of the carver as anything else. A person might have a pigeon engraved on their seal without having any particular fondness for, or association with, pigeons.

The seal image has drawn more than one Wallace biographer to questionable conclusions about the source of the experience that made Wallace a 'military genius'. It is quite possible that Wallace was a bowman of some skill and that his prowess as an archer was the inspiration for adopting an archery theme in his seal artwork. However, there is no evidence at all to lead us to believe that Wallace served Edward I in Wales in the campaigns there before 1296.

We might question the validity of describing Wallace as a 'military genius' at all. He was certainly an effective battlefield leader as the commander of a body of men-at-arms conducting hit-and-run operations against the English, and he was able to lead a large raiding force through the north of England, but the targets he found in Scotland were not primarily military ones so much as administrative operations. Wallace participated in only two large battles, Stirling Bridge and Falkirk. At the first of these the Scots took advantage of English indecision and disorganisation during a river crossing. The decision to attack may have rested with Wallace, but it may just as easily have been Andrew Murray who forced battle on the enemy. At his second battle, Falkirk, Wallace seems to have been caught by the unexpected approach of the English; he certainly seems to have had no clear plan for achieving victory over them.

If we are unsure of William Wallace's family, we are on even softer ground with some of his companions. Blair, the writer of the manuscript from which Blind Harry claimed to have made *The Wallace*, seems to have no provenance whatsoever as a historical figure, though that is hardly evidence of his non-existence. The same applies to Marion Braidfute. Just because there is no contemporary record of her life does not mean that she did not have one, though the absence of any other Braidfoots in the record material of the time would suggest that, if she did exist, her family was probably of very low status, low enough to avoid registering on the Ragman Roll. Alternatively, if Marion Braidfute never existed, it would not have been beyond the skills of a Scottish writer to invent her.

One of the few things we can safely say about William Wallace was that he was steadfast in his support of King John and the continuation of Scottish kingship independent of England. The fact that Wallace was able to furnish himself with armed support extensive enough to challenge the administration of Edward I within a matter of a few months of its establishment is indicative of more than an ability on the part of Wallace to motivate men. It suggests that there was a body of public opinion that was more than just receptive to appeals on behalf of the Balliol dynasty, but that was prepared, or even eager, to take up the fight.

It is easily forgotten that although the 1296 campaign had effectively been decided by the battle at Dunbar, the action had not been an extensive one. Only the Scottish noble cavalry, the men-at-arms of the army, and very probably only a proportion of those, had been engaged. There had been no great battle resulting in thousands of casualties among the infantry, the bulk of the army, which had simply disintegrated after Dunbar. The outcome of Falkirk may have made it harder for Scottish armies to recruit (though the evidence is hardly conclusive), but in 1297 the Scots had yet to experience a general engagement. Since most of the army of 1296 had not seen action, there is every reason to assume that many of them had retained the arms they had borne in that campaign and they had no reason to believe that the English could not be beaten in battle and ejected from the country.

Why exactly they should have chosen to enlist in the armies raised by Wallace, Murray, MacDuff of Fife or the 'Noble Revolt' of Bruce, the Stewart and Bishop Wishart at all is a complicated matter, and is addressed elsewhere, but the fact remains that Wallace was able to enlist men in considerable quantity.[5] His success in the minor actions that characterise Anglo-Scottish conflict in 1297 was undoubtedly a factor in attracting men to his banner, but, to some extent at least, there must have already been men who were willing to be lead. Wallace was their leader of choice, but we should not assume that they would not have been active in the Balliol cause had Wallace never existed. It is hardly likely that Wallace was able to single-handedly motivate large numbers of men to join in his venture if there was not already a body of opinion that was prepared to take action in favour of a restoration of the Balliol kingship, or, at the very least, the expulsion of the Plantagenet government. Nor is it likely that Wallace was the only man in Scotland trying to exert leadership in that direction, only that he was the most successful man of his station to do so. In the north-east, the fight against the occupation was taken up by a man of more exalted rank, Andrew Murray; in the south-west, by prominent magnates and prelates. In central Scotland, though, it was William Wallace who provided military leadership in the summer of 1297.

The earliest recorded operation of William Wallace was the murder of the sheriff of Lanark, Sir William Haselrigg,[6] allegedly in revenge for the murder of Wallace's mistress.[7] By May of 1297 he was the leader, with Sir William Douglas (father of the great Sir James, the original 'black' Douglas), of a group of men-at-arms, probably very small in number, that made a descent on the Plantagenet justiciar, William Ormsby, just as he was opening his court session at Scone, Perthshire. Ormsby escaped with his life, but there was no longer any question that a revolt against the occupation was under way.

In August 1297, at much the same time as Edward I was leaving England for Flanders, confident that he had dealt with the Scots, Wallace combined his army with that of Andrew Murray. As Dr Grant has observed, Wallace and Murray are among the small number of Scottish nobles that can be clearly identified as constant supporters of the Balliol cause and, in the case of the Murray family, with the continuation of the struggle under the Bruce party after 1306. Murray was a man of far greater status than Wallace, a man more in the tradition of noble political leadership, though not perhaps quite of the first rank. Murray had been made a prisoner of war in 1296,[8] presumably either at the Dunbar engagement or at the surrender of Dunbar Castle. He had subsequently escaped from captivity in an English castle and made his way north to raise men to fight against the occupation. His chief ally in the area was Alexander Pilche, a burgess of Inverness. Pilche has been seen as an example of the willingness of Scots of humble station to take up arms in the cause of independence; however, Pilche's status as a burgess was considerable. Only a very tiny proportion of the inhabitants of a burgh enjoyed the privilege of being members of the merchant or burgess guild which effectively provided the government of each burgh.[9] The high incidence of marriages between the families of lairds and burgesses is a clear indication of the social status of the latter.

Co-operation between the forces of Murray and Wallace had numerous clear benefits, both for their shared objectives and for the leaders as individuals. Obviously, the greater the force that could be raised and committed to operations against the occupation, the greater the chances of success, also, the fact of their co-operation would be likely to lend each a degree of credibility that they would not enjoy as separate operators. As the unchallenged commander of a large force and as a popular leader gaining a dramatic reputation, Wallace would have been a most attractive ally to Murray. As a prominent member of the Scottish political community, Murray might bring Wallace a degree of acceptance among the great and powerful men whose active support would be required if the occupation was to be defeated.

The majority of recruits were not in any sense experienced military men. The very low incidence of military activity of any kind in Scotland in the preceding fifty years meant that the opportunity to learn the skills and techniques of war, as opposed to personal ability at arms, had been, to say the least, limited. The most recent Scottish military operation had been the conquest of the kingdom of Man, an undertaking that had not stretched the capacities of even the very tiny Scottish military establishment, insofar as there was one at all. Without doubt, almost all of the men recruited by Wallace or Murray in 1297 served as spearmen and virtually all the remainder, though a small number, served as archers.

Historians of the period, for the best part of 100 years, have been quite clear that there was a distinction between

Scottish and English archers – the English used longbows and the Scots the less effective short bow.[10] To date, no actual evidence has been put forward to support this contention. If it was the case that Scots used the short bow, no medieval writer would seem to have noticed it, and it is certainly the case that the Scottish army operating in France in the 1420s included a large body of men armed with the longbow. There is a similar issue relating to the areas from which archers were recruited for Scottish armies. Contrary to a belief popular among medievalists, it was not the case that archers were drawn solely, or even particularly, from the forest of Ettrick. Several charters from the reign of Robert I or before specify the service of archers rather than men-at-arms. One of the heaviest military burdens in the whole of feudal Scotland outside the great lordships was an obligation to provide thirty archers for the king's army from the barony of Kilsyth.[11]

There was of course a great difference between an archer and a man who happened to be armed with bow and arrows, and there is no doubt that archery was more popular in England and enjoyed greater social status, at least in some areas. Men from Cheshire whose status would, in other counties, compel them to equip themselves and serve as men-at-arms can be identified serving as archers in France, Flanders and Scotland.

Since there were a great many archers in English armies the level of ability of each individual was not of greater importance – archery in battle was much more a matter of achieving high concentrations of missiles shot into a relatively small area than of marksmanship. The relative scarcity of archers in Scotland is probably more a reflection of the sizes of the respective populations. A very large English army in the late thirteenth or early fourteenth century might be as strong as 20,000 men. Of these, as many as 3,000 might be men-at-arms, a term which covered all those who served as heavy cavalry, from squires to the king himself. There might also another 1,000 or so less heavily armed and less well-mounted soldiers known as 'hobelars' who performed foraging and reconnaissance duties, but dismounted for combat in the event of a general engagement. Though this was not always the case – the army of 1314 does not appear to have had any cavalry element other than the men-at-arms. The balance of 17,000 would comprise spearmen and archers, mostly spearmen.

The first English army to treat the bow as a primary line-of-battle weapon was the one lead by Edward Balliol and Henry Beaumont to Dupplin Muir in 1332. There was certainly a sizeable contingent of archers in the English army defeated by Robert I at the Battle of Bannockburn, possibly as many as 3,000 or 4,000 out of an army in the region of 15,000 to 20,000 men, but there does not seem to have been anything that we could think of as a 'usual' or 'traditional' approach to the deployment of English armies until the adoption of massed archery as part of fundamental English practice in the 1330s and 1340s. Even the English armies that were consciously planned around the longbow seldom exceeded an archer strength of more than 4,000–5,000. Since the population of Scotland was a fraction of that of England, it is not surprising that the archer strength of their armies should be of the same order.

The same consideration applies to men-at-arms. The incidence of knight service or man-at-arms service does not seem to have been radically different to that in England relative to the populations. The small scale of cavalry service in Scottish armies can be very misleading, however. For one thing, men-at-arms, knights and lords might dismount to fight, depending on the tactical situation. Sir Edward Keith may have led a force of 500 mounted, armoured soldiers at Bannockburn, but that does not mean that King Robert's army was limited to 500 men-at-arms. Several of the most prominent Scottish knights of the day fought on foot there, including the Earl of Moray, the Stewart, Sir James Douglas, Angus Og MacDonald, Sir Neil Campbell and of course the king himself.[12] There was of course a political dimension to King Robert's choice to fight dismounted, the implication being that he would take his chance along with everyone else. The same applies to his declaration – according to Barbour – that he would refuse to be ransomed. Shakespeare ascribes a similar sentiment to Henry V on the eve of Agincourt. None of the prominent Scottish nobles fighting on foot at Bannockburn would have been alone among the common spearmen, but would have had a party of friends, relatives and tenants fighting alongside them.

There is a widely held belief that Scottish men-at-arms either could not or would not acquire the quality of mount or armament that their English counterparts enjoyed. If that was the case it was a matter that went unnoticed by English writers of the day, notably Sir Thomas Grey, who, like his father before him and his son after, made a career of army service in Scotland for Edward III and Edward Balliol.[13] By the time of Bannockburn, Scotland and England had been at war with one another for nearly twenty years, so it would be surprising if the Scots had not sourced the quality and quantity of equipment necessary to meet the English in battle and defeat them, but the horses and arms were available in Scotland in 1297. When Wallace and his followers raided Scone they were, so we are told, 'well-mounted', a phrase completely associated with men-at-arms and knights. Record strongly supports this – considerable numbers of Scottish men-at-arms and knights served in the Plantagenet garrisons wherever they existed, not just in the south and east as E.M. Barron implied.[14] They served on the same operational conditions as knights and men-at-arms from England or anywhere else, and were expected to have adequate mount and arms for heavy cavalry service.

Clearly the Scottish armies of the late thirteenth century could not field a force of men-at-arms as large as those raised by Edward I or his officers, but this was not simply a reflection of the larger and wealthier population of England. There was never a time when Wallace could call on the service of the entire political community of Scotland, which was the chief source of men-at-arms. In England or France the cavalry element of an army consisted of the retinues of the magnates. These retinues might be combined to form a number of stable formations for the duration of the campaign. A similar structure operated in Scotland, but not, perhaps, to the same extent. A very large part of the political community in Scotland consisted of relatively minor 'in capite' tenants, men who held their estates directly from the Crown rather than through an intermediary lord. There were, of course, very many people who did owe service to a superior lord, and these men formed the retinues of Scottish magnates on a similar, if not identical, pattern to their English counterparts. It would seem more likely than not that the minor 'in capite' tenants would have effectively fallen under the command of men with retinues, but it is possible that they were formed into units under officers appointed by the king or by the local sheriff.

However temporary the command arrangements might be, they must still have existed. The administration of a large body of men and horses would inevitably be something of a challenge. Maintaining an army is not simply a matter of keeping it fed, and even if it were, it would be virtually impossible to administer even that most basic function without some degree of articulation within the army – a means of dividing it into smaller formations than simply 'the army'.[15] The tactical need for a system of sub-division to allow manoeuvre on the battlefield is obvious, but would be necessary for the day-to-day existence of the army. The vital functions of gathering and distributing food and providing sentries and work parties would be very difficult to carry out without a means of apportioning suitably sized bodies of men to the tasks in hand.

The chronicler Walter Bower gives William Wallace the credit for introducing an articulated command system to the forces that he and Murray raised in the summer of 1297, but it would seem very unlikely that there had been no comparable system in the past. It could be argued that the previous system, if any existed, would have been discredited due to the Dunbar campaign of 1296. However, the Scottish infantry had not been engaged at Dunbar at all – it had not failed in battle. Whether the approach to command and control was good, bad or indifferent, it would at least have been fairly familiar to the men who joined Wallace and Murray. The arrangement described by Bower does seem to be a little fanciful, giving a very large proportion of the army some degree of authority over their peers, but it is not impossible. However, it is probably more realistic to assume that the structure was simpler, at least in lowest ranks, and that it pre-dated the army that fought at Stirling Bridge.

5

THE BATTLE OF STIRLING BRIDGE

The first question to be asked of any battle is, why should it have occurred at all? From the perspective of Edward I, the threat posed by Wallace and Murray to the English occupation was a challenge that could not possibly be ignored. Had Edward abandoned his Scottish ambitions, he would have had to abandon his garrisons and his adherents in Scotland, thus damaging his prestige as a soldier and a king and, in all probability, his financial situation – never a strong point with Edward I, since he would have faced a great deal of unrest from people who had been disadvantaged through their support for the Plantagenet cause.

Due to preparations for his expedition to the continent, Edward was not in a position to lead a force into Scotland himself in the summer of 1297, but even had he been able to do so, it is possible that he would still have left the operation in the hands of his lieutenants.[1] Had he been faced by a wider segment of the senior nobility obviously acting in concert, it might have been a different matter, but to react in person to the actions of a small group of magnates and two 'popular revolts' – one under a northern baron (or rather the son of a northern baron), Sir Andrew Murray, the other under the younger son of an obscure Ayrshire knight – could have given his enemies a certain credibility that might be denied them if all of the 'revolts' could be dealt with quickly and effectively through subordinates.

Edward had reasonably good cause to believe this would be a safe course of action – the Scottish nobility had already been humbled at Dunbar, little more than a year before, and he had no special reason to expect that the infantry element of a Scottish army would prove to be any more effective an opponent than the cavalry had. The Scottish men-at-arms at Dunbar had no real experience of war in 1296 and were easily outmanoeuvred and routed accordingly, but the majority of the man-at-arms class would seem to have escaped the battle unscathed.[2] The Scottish infantry had not been engaged at all at Dunbar, but had disintegrated in the wake of the rout of the cavalry and the surrender of Dunbar Castle. No doubt many of them abandoned arms and armour to facilitate a faster escape, but it would be unrealistic to assume that they all had, particularly those with a great distance to travel through a disturbed land to get home. It would be even more unreasonable to assume that any resulting shortage of arms could not have been made good in the period between Dunbar in the spring of 1296 and Stirling Bridge in the late summer of 1297.[3]

Wallace, and probably Murray as well, felt sufficiently short of men to enforce military service with the threat of the death penalty, but the majority of the men who followed either of them probably did so of their own free will. In the sense that all governments draw their power from the consent of the people, it is probably fair to say that Wallace and

Murray represented the most popular of the various groups competing for authority in Scotland by the midsummer of 1297 – Edward Plantagenet and the 'noble revolt' leaders Bruce, Wishart and the Stewart being the others.

The 'noble revolt' fizzled out in negotiations at Irvine, much to the detriment of the reputation of the men involved and the Scottish nobility in general. There are several issues to be considered, however. English chroniclers of the time seem to have believed that Bruce and Wishart stretched out the Irvine meeting as long as they possibly could to allow Wallace and Murray the best opportunity to assemble and train their men. It is certainly reasonable to assume that the number of men-at-arms that could be raised by Bruce, Wishart and the Stewart would have been very much smaller than that available to the Earl of Surrey. On the other hand, if Surrey had enjoyed a great superiority of numbers he could have forced battle on the Scots and undoubtedly have won the day. The fact that he did not suggests a number of possibilities. He may not have had an advantage in numbers, or not enough of an advantage for forcing battle to be a wise policy. Even with a substantial advantage, combat might not have been a desirable option. An English victory might not be successful in dissuading Scots from joining the Balliol cause if the English losses were comparable with the Scots, and an English defeat would probably help to dissuade Scots from actively supporting the Plantagenet government even if it did not encourage them to join the Balliol party. Even a sharp English victory might be counterproductive; it could harden attitudes among the Scots, particularly if it was followed by harsh retribution towards the participants. Perhaps most importantly, it may have been contrary to his instructions to bring about an engagement at all if he could avoid doing so.

Edward was well aware of the advantages of bringing the Scottish political community into his peace. As men who had exerted authority in their different regions, they were known to the community, the people were accustomed to accepting their leadership and, most importantly, they knew how the business of government was conducted in their locality – they would not inadvertently cause offence to the community by changing local practices. Moreover, in the short term at least, it would have been very difficult to maintain an administration at all without bringing some of the noble estate 'on board'. If none could be persuaded to uphold Plantagenet kingship, they would all have to be replaced if Edward's Scottish plans were to be made a reality.

Although there were doubtless plenty of men who would have been willing to undertake the role of laird, knight, baron or earl, there would have been very few with the necessary background to carry out the work properly, and many, probably most, of those people already had extensive estates elsewhere. They were hardly likely to abandon their properties in England in order to concentrate on making a reality of Scottish lordships granted by Edward, when the entire fabric of the Plantagenet government in Scotland might well be defeated.[4] If they were to make a worthwhile contribution to the administration or profit by Edward's grants – and the latter was obviously dependent on the security of the former – they would have to spend time in their new Scottish possessions to make good their lordship and to establish their authority with the tenants of the estates, a challenge in itself and a hopeless undertaking in areas outside Plantagenet control.

By the summer of 1297, Edward had been made aware that only a very small part of Scotland had been secured for his government and, more importantly, the Scots had restored pro-Balliol (or at least anti-Plantagenet) sheriffs and other officers in most of the counties that had been lost. Recovering those counties was likely to call for a huge investment in men, materials and money. The first two might be acquired through compulsion, though Edward was already less than popular at home, so demands for troops and supplies might not be a good move. As for the financial element, Edward was broke. If he could induce the Scottish nobles in the south-west to end their revolt without a clash of arms, his status as a wise and magnanimous lord would very probably be enhanced and there would be no need to raise any more troops for service in Scotland. Better still, he would have brought several Scottish magnates out of the enemy camp and into his own; he would have no need to install sympathetic leaders in the areas affected by the noble revolt, since they would now be his lords, not John Balliol's.

Regardless of whether the nobles made the Irvine negotiations a lengthy business for the benefit of Wallace and Murray (it is difficult to see what other cause they could have for doing so, and English writers seem to have been quite sure that they were taking their time), that was part of the outcome. That Wallace and Murray were able to raise troops at all seems to have come as a surprise to several historians, though not, seemingly, to observers at the time. They mention the activities and success of the Scots, but do not seem to have been at all surprised that a revolt had broken out, nor that the Scots were re-establishing government in the name of King John.

Self-evidently, Wallace and Murray were able to recruit men in considerable numbers, and, presumably, had embarked on a training programme more or less immediately, if only to help establish their authority. It would be rash to assume that they were the only men engaged in resistance to the Plantagenet government. Historians have seen that resistance as foolhardy in the face of Edward, the 'Hammer of the Scots', but in 1297 it was by no means clear that Edward was the 'hammer' of anybody other than the English nobility. His conquests in Wales were not yet completely secure, his wars with the French had hardly been an unalloyed success and his administration in Scotland was already close to complete collapse. The only clear battlefield victory that Edward had achieved was over those English barons who had continued to adhere to Simon de Montfort after Edward's own defection to his father's cause nearly forty years previously.[5]

Since the Scottish infantry had not fought at Dunbar, they had no reason to believe that they could not be victorious against the English, even if there had been extensive fighting in the period after Dunbar, and there is no evidence to suggest that there was, there had certainly not been any major confrontations in the period from then to Stirling Bridge. Despite the fact that there had been war for more than a year, there had been no great general engagement, only a clash between elements of the cavalry of both sides and an unknown number of minor skirmishes that probably owed as much to private enterprise – the line between political activity and banditry was a slender one – as anything else.

At some point in the summer of 1297, Wallace and Murray clearly came to an agreed policy with regard to the English. Instead of effecting a union of their armies at Stirling, they could have chosen to disperse the bulk of their troops and retain small mobile forces to harass the enemy until the problems of supply, pay and desertion forced him to withdraw.[6] Their decision to seek a confrontation suggests a number of issues that might have influenced them. The first is that they had come to the conclusion that they could win a battle if they could dictate the circumstances – if they had no confidence that their army could win a battle they would not have been willing to let the enemy come within striking range in the first place, but would have withdrawn. This does not imply that the Scottish commanders were sure of victory, or even that they were eager to offer battle at all, just that they believed that their force was competent for the purpose, should a good opportunity present itself. The army itself may well have exerted pressure in favour of combat; if Wallace and Murray were the inspirational leaders of tradition there would surely have been a highly charged and excitable element in the army that was desperately keen to fight.

The political situation certainly called for firm action, and combat must always be borne in mind by commanders as an option, however unpromising the immediate situation, but it would be unsafe to assume that the Scots were committed to accepting battle, let alone offering or forcing it. The Balliol party had made a remarkable recovery in 1296–97, but was still very vulnerable.[7] Most of Scotland north of the Forth was in Balliol control, or at least outside Plantagenet control, but the advent of a large English army might have been enough to undermine the credibility of the Balliol administration. If Wallace and Murray could prevent the English from crossing the Forth they would afford protection to the growing Scottish administration, but they did not necessarily have to give battle to achieve that end. An opposed river crossing has never been considered the easiest of operations to carry out. As long as the English could be denied adequate facilities for crossing the Forth at Stirling or below, their only real avenue to approach the Scots was to move upriver to find good fords, where, assuming the Scots matched the English movements, they would probably have to fight to effect a crossing – almost inevitably providing a good opportunity for the Scots to attack on advantageous terms.

The advantages that were likely to accrue from a success on the battlefield were substantial for either side. If Wallace and Murray could prevent the English from destabilising the Balliol administration, their stock as political entities would be very much enhanced; if they could actually defeat an English army, so much the better. Both Wallace and Murray were acting in a capacity more usually the province of kings and magnates. Murray was a relatively substantial lord, but Wallace was a political nonentity. He had neither lands nor office nor extensive experience of senior leadership. Although Wallace and Murray evidently enjoyed the confidence of the army – they had raised the men, after all – they had yet to establish themselves as a credible source of authority in a civil or political setting. On the eve of Stirling Bridge they could be described as the commanders of the Scottish army, but they were not yet acceptable to the bulk of the political community as the lieutenants of King John.

For the English commanders, combat was the only serious option unless the Scottish leadership was prepared to disband their army and throw themselves on the mercy of Edward I. The Scots might well be able to withdraw quickly enough into the north to avoid battle in the short term, but if Edward I was prepared (or could afford) to keep an army active in Scotland indefinitely, Wallace would have to give battle eventually or have his army melt away to nothing through a mixture of disillusionment and the demands of an agricultural economy – sooner or later, the men would want to go home to their families, farms and businesses.

Achieving complete victory over Wallace and Murray had a social and political significance for Edward I. A negotiated settlement with a small number of disaffected lords could be 'managed' with face-saving devices on both sides – a revolt of thousands under leadership that could be construed as a challenge to the traditional political order was a different matter. If Edward's administration were seen to be actively negotiating with Wallace and Murray, his prestige might be undermined and the great lords could claim to be acting in the interests of their country as the traditional representatives of their regions and in their traditional capacity of advisors to Scottish kings.

Neither Wallace nor Murray was a magnate and, therefore, their actions could be seen as undermining the authority of the magnates of Scotland as well as undermining the occupation government of King Edward. Additionally, the Balliol party had already made very rapid progress in installing an administration, and Wallace and Murray were obviously men capable of motivating thousands to join the struggle. If they, and the Balliol party generally, were not dealt with quickly, they might prove very hard to dislodge. Moreover, if they were successful in ejecting Edward's garrisons, his position at home might be undermined – his kingship was not particularly popular domestically with either the nobility or the commons of England. If the Plantagenet government was driven out of Scotland it might prove very difficult indeed to raise the men and money for an attempt at re-conquest, which, given that the Scots were now rather better organised for war, would probably be a much more difficult undertaking than the campaign of 1296. The English, then, were under some pressure to seek battle, and, in general terms, could be reasonably confident of the outcome; they had beaten the Scottish nobility at Dunbar and had encountered no serious opposition from the balance of the Scottish army through the following summer. There was very probably an element in the English army that doubted if the Scots would be prepared to fight at all.

The geographical location of Stirling has made it a focus for military activity throughout recorded history. As the first point at which the Forth could be crossed easily, possession of Stirling, or, strictly speaking, control of the bridge there, gave a great deal of control over access to Scotland north of the Forth. There were, and still are, several points above Stirling where the river could be crossed relatively easily on foot or horse, but few places which would allow passage by wagons. For an army to pass into northern Scotland it was necessary to secure a bridge crossing, so much so that Edward I commissioned a pontoon bridge to ensure that he would be able to effect a crossing even if he did not have possession of the bridge at Stirling.[8]

Although it has found a place in Scottish history books as the first great victory of the Scots over the English in the Wars of Independence, there was nothing inevitable about the process. Wallace and Murray united their forces to confront the English but whether or not they intended to offer, let alone provoke, battle is another question. They may have been looking for a confrontation, but that does not mean that they actually wanted a major engagement at all. If the English could be manoeuvred into a position that offered no good opportunities for attack, sooner or later they would be obliged to abandon their operation so long as the Scots stood fast.

Stirling offered just such a situation. If the Scots could maintain their position on the left bank of the Forth overlooking Stirling Bridge, it would be a very difficult proposition for the English to dislodge them. Given adequate logistic and financial support the English army could, in theory, wait for the Scots to grow tired of the business and drift off home. Unfortunately for the Earl of Surrey and Hugh Cressingham, this was not an option, even if they had wanted to adopt it. The financial position of Edward I's government was never really very good, but by the summer of 1297 it had been heavily burdened for many years and keeping a large army in place against the Scots was more of a burden than could be easily carried.

Money and food are always important issues for commanders, but they were not the sum of the challenges facing Cressingham. Virtually all medieval armies suffered from chronic desertion, the natural consequence of low pay, poor conditions and unpopular compulsory foreign service in a country from which one could make one's way home without having to board a ship. If desertion was high in English armies serving in France or Flanders, it must almost inevitably have been more of an issue for those serving in southern Scotland. Most of the men serving in Scotland for the Plantagenet cause in 1297 were recruited from the counties of northern England, making the journey home on 'unauthorised leave' not such a daunting project for a Durham soldier in Lothian or Roxburghshire as it would have been for a Cheshire man serving in France. Both might have to travel through hostile countryside, but the man deserting from army service in Scotland could at least walk home.

The spectre of desertion and the pressing difficulties of supply and pay were not the only factors that pushed the

English to a combat option. Edward I was not going to be at all impressed if Cressingham failed to force battle on the Scots, particularly in the light of the successful negotiated settlement that had just been made with the leaders of the 'noble revolt' at Irvine. Having taken an army to meet the enemy, it would have been very detrimental to Edward's regal prestige if there was no significant victory to compensate for the costs. If the English failed to engage at all, it would undoubtedly give a moral – or perhaps morale – advantage to the Balliol cause while simultaneously undermining the credibility of the occupation government, whose authority rested solely on success in war. For the Scots, then, battle was not strictly necessary for victory. If they could confront the English army at Stirling for long enough without giving battle they could achieve a tactical and political victory without any loss whatsoever. This was presumably clear to Cressingham, an intelligent and experienced political operator.

In addition to the political imperatives that made battle a preferred policy, there were practical martial issues. As well as having to weather the reaction of Edward I to a failure to carry the war to the Scots, if Cressingham decided to take his army home the desertion rate would very likely rise rather than fall. Men would be inclined to feel that their personal contribution was not going to make any difference to the situation and that they might as well make the journey home faster rather than slower, thus weakening the army at a potentially alarming rate at a point when it was being shadowed by the Scots. Wallace and Murray might be prepared to let the English depart in peace, but it is surely much more probable that they would take every opportunity to harass the English retreat, and might even be able to inflict a defeat on Cressingham's army during its return to England. If Cressingham's own estimate of the strength of his force is to be accepted at face value then he only had 300 men-at-arms in an army of 10,000,[9] a very weak mounted element for an army on the march. The Scots would have been able to match a man-at-arms element of that stature without much difficulty, though traditionally that was a weak aspect of Scottish armies throughout the Middle Ages. Cressingham's assessment of his numerical strength was not, however, made at Stirling, but at Roxburgh, more than a fortnight before the battle. His command had almost certainly been weakened by desertion and disease over the intervening period.

At least one writer has suggested that Cressingham's army could not have amounted to 10,000 foot, partly on the grounds that Edward himself led a smaller army on the continent and partly due to exaggeration on the part of Cressingham; however, there was no advantage to be had in telling King Edward that his army was greater than it actually was. The greater the army, the more Edward would expect his lieutenant to achieve with it. If anything, it would have been in Cressingham's interest to understate his strength rather than overstate it. The size of Edward's army is, in any case, completely irrelevant to the size of Cressingham's force – they were two different armies raised for different theatres.

Desertion may have reduced the infantry element of the English army, but probably had little impact on the men-at-arms. It was by no means unknown for men-at-arms to desert, but it was certainly very much less common, chiefly because they were easier to identify and therefore prosecute when the opportunity arose. Because of the rather better pay and conditions and because of the cultural mores of the late thirteenth century, men of rank and status were expected to pay for their privileged position in society through service to the Crown, but it was also something of a social imperative. In a society which liked to think that it adhered to the values of chivalry, fighting was a natural part of social, political and cultural identity.

The 300 men-at-arms that Cressingham had under command at Roxburgh may not have been the total extent of his cavalry arm. Scottish nobles and burgesses who had appended their seals to the Ragman Roll and had remained in Edward's peace owed exactly the same level of military obligation to King Edward as they had to King John or to Alexander III. No record has survived relating to the service of Scottish men-at-arms serving Edward I at Stirling Bridge, but it is highly probable that the occupation government would have made some effort to call on that service. Not only was the service itself desirable, but activity on behalf of the English Crown had a political dimension. If the Scots nobility could be induced to fight for Edward I, that would deny their service to the Balliol party, a useful objective.

Superficially, Cressingham was in a very advantageous position. The collapse of the 'noble revolt' had removed one threat to the occupation and a successful operation at Stirling would very probably undermine the other fatally. With a little good fortune he would be able to destroy Wallace and Murray and then penetrate northern Scotland. In practice, Cressingham really had little choice other than to fight. Had Cressingham chosen to withdraw, he would have faced the prospect of what would inevitably have been a very difficult interview with his king. Edward had no great opinion of the Scots generally, and would not be impressed in the slightest by the issues faced by his lieutenants in Scotland. Edward wanted results, and quickly, before the Scots could establish their authority at home or attain any degree of international political credibility.

Practically, his situation was rather more precarious. He has been criticised, and rightly, for failing to take advantage of local knowledge which might have allowed him to make a flanking move on the Scottish position, but that would be rather dependent on managing to make a crossing farther upstream. It might have been possible for Richard Lundie, a Scottish knight who had defected to the English at Irvine in his disgust at the ineffectiveness of the Scots, to take the 500 men-at-arms he asked for across the river at Drip Fords or elsewhere, but it was not guaranteed; he might well have had to make an opposed river crossing in the face of superior numbers. His proposal may not have been a practical proposition anyway. If there were as many as 500 men-at-arms in the English army they must have come from other sources beyond the army that Cressingham had mustered at Roxburgh, since Cressingham was clear that he had only 300 men-at-arms in his command there. It is quite possible that this was the case. As we have already seen, Scots in English peace who had a military obligation would have been under some pressure to discharge their obligation to the 'new administration' of Edward I just as they had been under Scottish kings, so there may have been a contingent of such men from those counties most securely held by the English: Lothian, Roxburghshire, Lanarkshire, Berwickshire, Peeblesshire and Dumfriesshire.

It is not clear whether Cressingham's force of 300 men-at-arms present at Roxburgh included the force that Clifford and Percy had commanded at Irvine, but it must be considered unlikely. Clifford's force had been enough to dissuade the 'noble revolt' leaders into seeking terms. There is no reason to assume that he led a particularly large force at

Irvine, but it must surely have been a body powerful enough to convince the Scots that battle was out of the question. Although the 'noble revolt' did not attract many of the great lords of Scotland, it is ludicrous to imagine that the leaders of the revolt were prepared to even consider a confrontation with the English unless they too had a significant force.

The pressure on Wallace and Murray to give battle was not as well developed as that on Cressingham, but it was still an issue. Although their authority would be bolstered if Cressingham withdrew, they must have been aware that a battlefield victory would be better for their political and military status than any other outcome. The men who joined the armies of Wallace and Murray did so in order to fight and win, not to stand on the Ochil Hills waiting for the enemy to march off home. If the campaign of summer 1297 failed to achieve significant results under the leadership of Wallace and Murray, they might find it very difficult indeed to recruit an army for the campaign of 1298 – what was the point of giving military service if it did not bring easily recognisable benefits? Wallace and Murray had to protect their credibility as leaders. In one sense at least this was more of a difficulty than it was for Edward, since he had the benefit of kingship, a matter of status as well as of political power. Edward inherited authority, whereas Wallace and Murray had to acquire it, and in August 1297 their status as leaders was completely dependent on maintaining the military initiative. It was not crucial for them to offer battle in the short term, but wars are seldom won without trials of arms. Sooner or later they would have to fight unless Edward was willing to abandon his ambitions in Scotland, a very unlikely circumstance.

The popular perception of the battle, unusually, is not far removed from the reality; even some of the more

dubious assertions of the chroniclers may in fact be fundamentally sound. The initial activities of the day as recorded
by Walter of Guisborough would seem to beggar belief,
but are not perhaps quite as unlikely as they would appear.
According to Guisborough, the English army initiated two
premature crossings of the bridge before the battle proper
began. The first formations to cross did so at dawn but
were quickly recalled, due to the fact that the other significant English commander, the Earl of Surrey, was still
in his bed. Though not impossible, this has to be considered rather suspect. Even if true, his fondness for his sleep
would not have been a good reason to recall the men who
had already crossed. Since the troops started to cross at
dawn, it is perfectly possible that the business of waking
troops and putting them into march order before first light
had not been a great success, leading to a bottleneck at the
bridge itself but also, very probably, to a good deal of general confusion among the English army. With the majority
of the army still being marshalled on the south bank of
the river, the balance of the army on the north side would
be very vulnerable to a sudden Scottish attack. Even if the
Scots were heavily outnumbered, and there is no great
weight of evidence to indicate that they were, they might
well be able to achieve local superiority on the north bank
while the rest of the English army looked on ineffectually
from the south bank.

The second alleged crossing commenced rather later in
the morning, but, again according to Guisborough, was
recalled because of the arrival of some Scottish magnates in
the English camp, bearing news that Wallace and Murray
were prepared to negotiate. An agreed settlement would
have been an attractive proposition for Cressingham.
Even if he were to inflict a massive defeat on Wallace

and Murray there was no guarantee that they, or others, would not continue to oppose the Edwardian occupation. However, if the Scots could be induced to disband their army he would have achieved a political victory that might go some way toward disarming the Balliol cause more generally. He may have believed, with some justification, that this was exactly what had already occurred at Irvine, with very positive results for the administration – Robert Bruce and the Stewart were now in the Plantagenet party, so why should Wallace and Murray not be brought into Edward's peace? If they were, the leadership and credibility of the Balliol cause would be dealt a major blow and, assuming that Wallace and Murray did disband their army, Cressingham would be able to lead his army across the Forth and into northern Scotland, where he could set about dismantling whatever was left of the Balliol administration without fear of serious opposition.

Cressingham might have been prepared to consider negotiations, but it is not at all clear that Wallace or Murray were interested in the slightest. Cressingham would never have been willing to entertain the notion that he could withdraw his army and abandon the remaining administrators and garrisons (King Edward would not have given him the authority to do), so really he had nothing to offer to the Balliol party other than terms for their surrender or battle. Nonetheless, if there was any possibility of agreement Cressingham would have been unwise not to pursue it. If Guisborough's assertion that the Stewart approached Cressingham with an offer of discussions at a point when only part of the English army had crossed the bridge is true, he might well have felt that it was preferable not to leave a portion of his army exposed to the possibility of a sudden attack from the Scots. The situation would have been very similar to that which had already occurred (according to Guisborough) earlier in the day.

Although negotiations would have held some attraction for Cressingham, he did have good cause to believe that combat would be to his advantage. The Scots were evidently very weak in men-at-arms and in any case, since the fight at Dunbar the previous spring, English commanders generally had little reason to be impressed by the performance of Scottish cavalry. The Scottish command consisted of two men – in itself a situation traditionally considered unwise – neither of whom had, so far as we are aware, any extensive experience of making war, and the Scottish army largely comprised men who had never seen a major action. The level of experience among his own troops may not have been very much greater than that of the Scots, but Cressingham still had good cause to believe that his army was the superior, in quality certainly and probably in quantity as well. The Scottish cavalry had been routed easily and quickly at Dunbar and the Scottish infantry had yet to meet the English in battle at all.

A good deal has been written about the nature of the relationship between Wallace and the nobility, one writer going so far as to assert that the Wallace/Murray plan for battle was '… largely improvised, and was the work of men of a different mentality from the lords' but neglecting to inform the reader about the manner in which Wallace and Murray differed from the rest of the members of their class.

Wallace's early actions all seem to carry the hallmarks of traditional and conventional military practice of the day: he led a party of men-at-arms. That was, however, only part of the tradition of medieval war. The belief among historical enthusiasts that the infantry were not thought to be an important part of the structure of an army seems very curious indeed, considering that very few medieval armies of manoeuvre were anything less than 70 per cent infantry, and more usually of the order of 80 or even 90 per cent. If the infantry were insignificant, why were they recruited at all? Wallace, Murray, Edward I, Cressingham and Surrey all seem to have been convinced that a strong force of infantry was a vital part of the structure of their armies.

The course of the engagement at Stirling Bridge is not the subject of any great amount of historical controversy, which is in itself something of a rarity in medieval war studies. Cressingham's decision to cross the river cannot be seen in any other light than an attempt to force battle on the enemy. The Scots kept to their position until a body of the enemy army had effected a crossing, before making a rapid descent on them from the area to the west of the Wallace monument. There would appear to have been no requirement for manoeuvre, though at least one recent commentator has decided, for reasons that he has not chosen to divulge, that the Scottish army made an oblique manoeuvre in the course of advancing to contact. Such a movement would have been very difficult to achieve, as well as unnecessary if the Scots had adopted a position that would prevent an English force from advancing northwards after crossing the river.

Naturally, it is reasonable to assume that Wallace and Murray made a deliberate choice to attack: their enemy was, after all, in a very vulnerable position. However, it is always possible that they in fact had to make the best of a bad job. Some portion of the Scottish army is likely to have been very keen indeed to get into action, and, if Guisborough is correct in his description of the English army as making three separate attempts to cross the bridge, there must have been a degree of excitement among the troops: they had seen the enemy cross and retire twice. When the English made their third attempt it is likely that Wallace, Murray and their subordinates would have struggled to prevent a general advance even if they had wanted to. The opportunity was, however, far too good to miss, and whether the Scots made a precipitate and unauthorised advance or whether Wallace and Murray gave the order for it is not too important – what mattered was the outcome.

The area into which the leading English units debouched when they crossed the bridge was not very extensive. The 'buckle' of the Forth meant that they had deployed into a near-circular area bounded by a river too fast, too wide and too muddy to cross, with a very narrow 'neck' from which the English would have to advance on the Scots. The problem of course was that the Scots did not wait to be attacked, but made a descent on the English that effectively blocked up the 'neck', denying the English the space to deploy properly and forcing the English back on their supports. Due to the narrowness of the bridge, the English could not join the fight.

As ever with a medieval battle, it is difficult, if not impossible, to come to any realistic conclusions about casualties. The Scottish chroniclers are very clear that Scottish casualties were very light indeed, but that is of course to be expected. The lack of a great list of prominent gentlemen killed or taken prisoner should not be seen as an indication that the Scottish army was unscathed by the battle. The most significant casualty on the Scottish side was, of course, Sir Andrew Murray. He was not killed in the action, but died of his wounds some weeks later. Self-evidently Murray had taken part in the battle, as had Wallace.

Personal combat by commanders was part of the nature of medieval battle, and Stirling Bridge was not exceptional in that regard: Murray was fatally wounded, Cressingham was killed and William Wallace no doubt behaved as gallantly as chroniclers would have us believe. Personal prowess at arms was an important aspect of medieval leadership; example was considered important, but the efforts of one man, however strong, brave, skilled and determined, are still only the efforts of one man.

The William Wallace who took part in the Battle of Stirling Bridge bears little, if any, resemblance to the giant warrior beloved of popular writers. A recent writer tells us that Wallace cleaved his way through the English wielding the vast sword that can be seen today at the Wallace monument. Apart from the fact that two-handed swords the better part of 6ft long were not a feature of the medieval arsenal generally, the sword in question is a much later artifact, probably from the late fifteenth or early sixteenth century, and therefore has no connection with William Wallace's life whatsoever. Wallace the warrior, casting about him with a great cleaver, scattering the English before him in a welter of amputated arms, legs and heads, may be an attractive romantic picture, but not a useful one. There is no reason to believe that William Wallace was given to fighting in any mode other than the one he grew up with, that of a conventional armoured, mounted soldier of the late Middle Ages – a man-at-arms. In close combat, the life expectancy of a man-at-arms without a shield would have been very short indeed and it is extremely difficult to see how a man could use a two-handed sword and a shield at the same time. The two-handed sword only became viable for men-at-arms when body armour had developed to a degree that made a shield more of a burden than it was worth[10] and was in any case an option for dismounted action, not for fighting on horseback.

The outcome of the action was certainly dramatic, probably exceeding the very best hopes of Wallace and Murray. They probably had little doubt about the prospect of victory once battle was joined. The tactical situation suited them well and they must have had some confidence in their troops, otherwise they would have avoided the risk of a major engagement, but the political results were as significant as the military, possibly more so. With a major success behind them, Wallace and Murray could not be ignored as political figures. To what extent the Guardianship was entrusted to them and to what extent they simply assumed the role is impossible to say. Unsurprisingly, the magnates of Scotland did not leave any record of their reaction to the political advancement of a minor baron and an obscure member of the lesser nobility. Stirling Bridge had seriously undermined the security of the occupation government and proved that the English in arms were not invincible, but it had also brought a prominence to Wallace and Murray that was rare for men of their station in society.

If victory on the battlefield brought political advancement for Wallace and Murray, it did not bring the war to a close, and the new Guardians would have to establish their authority and prove that they were worthy of their office. Murray's role in government was of course very brief; he died – probably of his wounds – a few weeks after the battle, leaving Wallace to carry on as sole Guardian. For a short while at least, Wallace was probably able to proceed as he saw fit without any great amount of consultation or consideration of the peacetime political community, but it is hard to accept that he was able to carry on the business of government without the support of a considerable portion of that community – their participation in the administration of justice and the collection of issues and military service was a vital prop to any party aspiring to power.

Although there is very little in the way of documentation showing the Wallace government at work, there can be little doubt that there was plenty to do. The management of the war must surely have taken priority over civil issues, but the latter could not be ignored. As a substitute for the king, Wallace would have been the recognised source of authority in the Balliol camp, and as such he would have had to fulfil the functions of kingship other than war. After 11 August 1297, William Wallace the soldier had to become William Wallace the politician.

His ideological position was not a complicated one. As Guardian his responsibility extended into every sphere of the life of the community – war, justice and the economy. To a considerable degree, his interest in the last of these was related to the first. Wallace and Murray's letters to German merchants at Hamburg and Lubeck[11] did have a political/diplomatic dimension. Wallace was looking for international recognition of the existence of a Scottish polity and of his rule within that polity, but the economic aspects relating to the war were pressing issues. Although arms and armour of all kinds could be, and were, manufactured in Scotland,[12] it is reasonable to assume that the demand for arms had increased dramatically in 1295–96 as relations between England and Scotland deteriorated, and that the existing Scottish manufacturers and suppliers could not hope to satisfy that demand. The repeated instructions from English kings to their own subjects (and, through their fellow rulers, to the subjects of others) to refrain from exporting war materials generally, and arms and armour in particular, to Scotland is a clear indication that the arms trade into Scotland was exceptionally profitable – sufficiently so for merchants to feel it was worth risking their ships, not to mention the extreme displeasure of their king, in the search for a fast return on investment.[13]

Naturally, arms had to be paid for, and the purchase of foreign arms meant the export of goods to finance arms procurement. To what extent, if at all, Wallace's government bought arms for distribution to their soldiers is not known. The normal practice of war throughout Europe called for the personal ownership of weapons, armour and horses. However, that does not preclude the possibility that 'munition'[14] weapons were acquired so that more infantry could be enlisted. In 1332, during his first attempt at gaining Scottish kingship, Edward Balliol's army apparently uncovered a cache of spears, variously reported as 800 or 4,000.[15] The second figure would represent a huge arsenal, but even the lesser one would have been a substantial investment. These spears may have been bought by the Crown either for issue or for sale to the troops, but they were certainly bought against the eventuality of war; there is no reason to assume that the Wallace government was not capable of doing the same thing.

Apart from the conduct of the war generally, there were other issues that required Wallace's attention. Primarily, reducing the garrisons of the occupation government and replacing the Plantagenet sheriffs and bailies (local administrators) with men of his own choice, and also campaigning for the allegiance of areas that remained in English control.

A good deal has been written in the past about the letters Wallace sent from Haddington to Lubeck and Hamburg, but little about the circumstances that took Wallace to Haddington in the first place. The strong castles of Lothian made the business of maintaining an occupation government there less of a challenge than in other parts of the country. It has long been the opinion of many English and Scottish historians that the Lothian community was actually perfectly content with English administration (though the evidence to support that position is, to say the least, thin on the ground) and there is no doubt that, in comparison to most other Scottish counties in 1297–98, Lothian was held relatively securely for the Plantagenets. This may not have been quite so clear to the English administration there at the time. At least three Lothian castles[16] had been recovered from the English before the Battle of Falkirk and in November 1297 Wallace had led his army into what was – supposedly – an area where the English administration was intact.

Marching into Lothian was an operation with several dimensions. As the Guardian, Wallace had to give some proof of his commitment to eventually recovering the entirety of Scotland for King John, not just the parts of it from which the English could be dislodged easily. One aspect of that was simply the business of carrying the war to the enemy – the Lothian campaign certainly did that. Another was to establish his lordship among the Scots generally and in Lothian itself in particular. In short, the 1297 campaign was a mixture of flag-waving, sabre-rattling, crowd-pleasing and a less than subtle threat to the Lothian political community. By marching through the country in force, Wallace demonstrated his power to friends, foes and falterers alike. People sympathetic to the Balliol cause could be encouraged in their loyalty by the visible presence of a Scottish army; those inclined toward the Plantagenets were likely to be discouraged by the fact that Wallace could march his troops around the country with seeming impunity; and the people of Lothian were likely to become rather focused on their own futures. Wallace's arrival in Lothian was a boost to his supporters, but it was also an indication that those who sided with the occupation might have to explain their actions to a restored Balliol king at some point in the future, possibly quite soon. The success of the Lothian campaign was quite limited, however.

The castles that fell to the Scots may well have been turned over to the forces of William Wallace by their garrisons or just plain abandoned; there is no evidence to indicate that they fell to siege or storm. The central establishment of the English administration in Lothian, Edinburgh Castle, does not seem to have been threatened at all. Although the garrison was small, the castle was very strong indeed and was unlikely to fall without a protracted siege. The presence of Wallace's army would have deterred the garrison from mounting operations against the Scots and, temporarily, from fulfilling the other roles of such installations – gathering rents and other dues and maintaining law and order – but Wallace was not able to put his own officials in place with any confidence. He might be able to lead an army into Lothian and march it out again without intervention by the English, but he had not brought Lothian back under Scottish control for King John. That does not mean that the Lothian campaign was a failure; in all likelihood Wallace did not expect to recover the sheriffdom in one operation. Even if he had been able to win the unswerving allegiance of all of the Lothian communities to the Balliol cause, he did not have the material or expertise to conduct one conventional siege, let alone invest all of the smaller strongholds held for the Plantagenet cause throughout the sheriffdom.

Wallace's offensive into Lothian would have brought some recruits to the Balliol party through demonstrating that the issue of independent Scottish kingship was not a lost cause, but he could not afford to enforce his authority through the sheriffdom by military power. If he kept his army in Lothian he would have to feed it from the resources of the county, a burden that would almost inevitably draw local sympathies to the Plantagenets. Nonetheless, if William was to keep a force in being through the winter, it would have to be fed. Obviously it would be better for William's reputation if he could maintain the army without imposing on Scottish communities other than for manpower, and it would be better for the army if it was kept busy with worthwhile operational activity rather than idling in billets through the winter, a sure-fire recipe for disorder. These considerations made an invasion of England an attractive proposition militarily, but there was an important political dimension as well. Wallace's prestige and credibility as Guardian rested firmly on his success in arms against the English. If he did little or nothing for even a few months, the lustre of his achievements was liable to fade quickly, possibly leading to competition for the Guardianship from men of greater social rank. A successful foray south of the border would go a long way toward confirming his political position among the Scottish hierarchy and maintaining his popularity and authority in the army.

6

FROM VICTORY
TO IGNOMINY

If Stirling Bridge gave Wallace power, it also gave him responsibility. He was not the king, but he did have the authority – given or assumed – to wield the royal prerogative. His political role as the king's substitute would have involved a great variety of activities, but military affairs naturally formed a significant portion of his duties. The greatest priority was obviously the army. In the winter of 1297 he led his army into England.

Unlike Edward I's invasion of Scotland, Wallace's invasion of England was not mounted to secure territory, but to undermine the authority of Edward I and to enhance his own prestige as Guardian.[1] It also gave him the opportunity to feed his army at the expense of his enemy. His approach was not revolutionary; at the beginning of hostilities in March 1296 the Scots had mounted a series of raids into northern England, presumably to demonstrate that a state of war existed and thereby fulfil the commitment of John I to his treaty obligations with Philip IV of France. These operations do not seem to have had any very specific military objectives – no English castles or towns were seized and English landholders were not pressured to give their allegiance to King John. The achievements of the Scots in England in 1296 were limited to the diplomatic obligations of the Scoto–French treaty of 1295[2] and some indiscriminate looting and burning.

After Stirling Bridge Wallace set himself to the task of pressing on with the war. The fact that he could do this would seem to support the possibility that he had either been able to assume control of the Scottish admin-istration, which was already recovering and appointing officials by the summer of 1297, or that he had effec-tively been adopted by the active elements of the political communities of Scotland as an acceptable leader in the absence of the king. He was of course active in spheres other than warfare.

On 11 October 1297 Wallace was at Haddington, with sufficient force to deter the English garrisons of Lothian from confronting him.[3] The garrison commanders may have been aware that Wallace intended to move on quickly from Haddington and therefore may have been unwilling to risk any operations at all if Wallace was about to leave their area of responsibility. They may have simply been keen to avoid a fight; the English had, after all, been beaten at Stirling just a few weeks before. Wallace was unable to seize Edinburgh, town or castle, but it would be unrealis-tic to assume that he simply ignored the English garrisons in Lothian, Lanark and Roxburghshire as he made his way to England. Although he could not have had many men-at-arms to spare to counter the garrison forces, the garrison complements were not large,[4] and could prob-ably be contained within their establishments by relatively small numbers of men. He evidently was not too concerned about the garrisons in Scotland since he was prepared to undertake an invasion of England.

Under normal circumstances, mounting an operation into England would have been a very risky business, but the circumstances were not normal. The knights and men-at-arms that served in the English army at Stirling Bridge would have been drawn from the political communities of the north of England, particularly Northumberland and Cumbria.[5] Since a large number of these men were either dead or captives of the Scots or were serving in Scotland anyway, the English military establishment of northern England was deprived of a significant portion of its armoured cavalry strength and, perhaps more importantly, it's political and military leadership. These men were not just the striking arm of the northern English army, they were the men who would normally ensure that military service was being discharged, both by the other members of the political community and by the rest of the population. In a sense, their skills and experience were secondary considerations. What was important was that the community knew who they were and that they held the appropriate authority. Naturally the men who had been killed or captured at Stirling Bridge had sons or brothers to take their places in military activity, but the mere fact that there were a lot of new faces would not have been an encouragement to any forces raised to oppose the Scots in the autumn of 1297. The situation was, perhaps, similar to that in Scotland in the spring and summer of 1296. The actual number of men killed or taken prisoner at Dunbar was not particularly large, but it did include a significantly large proportion of the leadership of the Balliol party.[6]

The absence of any realistic attempt to confront the Scots in October and November 1297 is not adequately explained by the casualties at Stirling Bridge. The political communities of Westmorland and Northumberland had been damaged, but not those of the other northern counties. The military tenants of Lancashire, Cheshire and Yorkshire had not taken part in the Stirling Bridge campaign. The fact that they had been on active service in Scotland before that[7] did not, however, excuse them from their obligation to serve against invasion, yet there seems to have been no co-ordinated effort to raise a force of men-at-arms from these counties. One explanation may lie in an unwillingness to abandon home and hearth, thus allowing the Scots to penetrate into these counties unopposed. The plight of the people of Northumberland might not seem so critical to Yorkshiremen if there was any chance at all of a Scottish army turning up outside York.

If there was no co-ordinated plan among those responsible for military leadership in northern England, it would seem that there was no real agenda among the Scots either. Colm MacNamee has put forward the possibility the Wallace did not in fact instigate the invasion of England at all, suggesting that Scots acting on their own initiative were active in Northumberland by 13 October 1297, though Wallace himself had still been at Haddington two days before. Whether he directed an assault on northern England as a matter of policy or whether he assumed control of a situation that he could not prevent, Wallace does not seem to have been able to exercise much control over his men compared to the discipline that Robert I was able to impose on his armies in similar circumstances a generation later, but, like Robert, he seems to have lacked the resources to mount an effective siege. He approached Newcastle and Carlisle, but made no attempt to take either, though he may have been able to contain the garrison at Carlisle and prevent them from hindering his operations in the area.

The Scots would seem to have been perceived as a threat, if not yet a reality, by 15 October, when the local clergy voted money for military preparations[8] and in London orders for a muster were issued, though it was not to take place until 6 December, some six weeks distant.[9] Although communications were slow in the Middle Ages, and administrative functions sometimes cumbersome, six weeks does not seem to indicate any sense of urgency on the part of the English government. It would surely have been possible to give suitable authority to an officer of the Crown and entrust that person with making an appropriate response to the Scots; however, the timing of the muster may have been a conscious policy decision based on an estimate of the resources available to William Wallace, rather than on those available to the English Crown. By the time an English army assembled on 6 December, Wallace's army would have been operating continuously for much longer than the traditional forty days' service owed to the Crown. Service in Scotland could be extended, in theory anyway, almost indefinitely, since there was an obvious threat to the security of the country as long as there was an English military presence.[10] Service against the English outside Scotland may have been a rather harder proposition to 'sell' to the Scots as part of their customary obligation. With any luck – from an English point of view – by the time the army was on the march Wallace's force would have dwindled in quantity, and probably in quality as well. The men whose service was most vital to the Scottish cause were the men who could afford to invest in appropriate horses and equipment; however, to a considerable extent these were inevitably the men whose presence was most needed on the 'home front'. They were the farmers, minor landholders, merchants and craftsmen on whom the economy rested. The men who were willing to serve continually were more likely to be men with little in the way of means other than the army or prospects other than plunder.

William Wallace led his men around northern England for five weeks before returning to Scotland. In a sense it was an aimless exercise, a meandering around Northumberland, Cumbria and Westmorland, doing very little beyond ruining farms and villages, but achievements of the 1297 campaign were real, if transitory. The Scottish army had been maintained for several weeks on the enemy's territory and had taken large quantities of plunder and provisions back to Scotland in a year of poor agricultural yields all over northern Europe.[11] Scottish morale would certainly have been improved by news of a successful foray against the English, and the prestige of William Wallace as Guardian of the realm would have been enhanced accordingly. All the same, no blow of political significance had been landed. To an extent, the Scots could regard that as a victory in itself: they had invaded the king of England's realm, despoiled it, and returned home unscathed. More realistically, the English political position was untouched. The Scots could not force Edward to the negotiating table by burning the homes and farms of his northern subjects.

Wallace could not keep his army in the north of England indefinitely. Once the land had been swept of movable goods and standing crops and byres fired, he had to move on, but he could not afford to move any further south for fear of having his return journey barred by a force raised in his rear. By Christmas Wallace was back in Scotland and the English were already mounting a recovery in Berwickshire and Roxburghshire[12] thus relieving any immediate pressure on the Plantagenet administration in Lothian.

Preparations for a major invasion to restore the fortunes of the English in Scotland were not undertaken until the return of Edward I from Flanders in March 1298. It had become all too plain that the Scots would have to be taken seriously, and the army raised for the purpose would have to be the product of a major effort. The force commanded by Cressingham at Stirling Bridge had not been insignificant, but it had obviously not been adequate to the task. The man-at-arms element had been small and the army does not seem to have been well organised. The army of 1298 was larger, better resourced and, perhaps most importantly, was led by King Edward himself. The army he summoned was a powerful one – writs were issued for the enlistment of over 10,000 men from Wales and a further 1,000 each from Cheshire and Lancashire.[13] The other northern counties, Northumberland, Westmorland, Cumbria and Durham, were not called upon to provide contingents of infantry, though several knights and men-at-arms from those communities joined the army as it passed northwards. To some extent this may have been a recognition of their sufferings of the previous year; however, it also meant that there was a reservoir of manpower in those counties should Wallace manage to evade Edward and cut his communications or make another foray into England.

The heavy cavalry element of the army amounted to something over 2,000 men-at-arms[14] and knights, of whom slightly more than 50 per cent were serving for royal wages, the balance being provided by the retinues of the magnates attending the king. Even for the wealthiest of the great lords and earls, leading a retinue in the king's army was an expensive business. Some portion, possibly a very large one, of the men in his command would have been discharging the obligations attached to their landholdings, or would have been provided at their expense if they could not serve in person; others, however, would require wages and indemnification for loss of horses and perhaps for losses incurred by being captured and ransomed. All would expect to be shown some sign of appreciation during or after the campaign.

King Edward arrived at York with the household element of the army on 16 May 1298. On the assumption that there would be a brief campaign, Edward moved his seat of government to York as a temporary measure to ease the administration of the war. It would continue to be the principal seat of his government for the next six years while he tried to bring the Scottish war to a satisfactory conclusion. From York he marched to Durham, arriving on 12 June and resting there some time before moving on to Newcastle. By the middle of July he was at Temple Liston, waiting for supplies and mounting relatively minor operations against the Scots, such as detaching the bishop of Durham, Antony Bek, to recover three castles in Lothian lost to the Scots over the preceding year.

King Edward was in a difficult situation in July 1298. His supply arrangements had broken down badly through a mixture of unseasonable weather conditions and a shortfall in promised shipping. There can be little doubt that desertion was already an issue in the army; if Edward could not feed the troops it would increase. When supplies were eventually landed and delivered to the army, matters went from bad to worse – the chief part of the delivery was wine and within a short time a major riot broke out between Welsh and English infantrymen.[15]

Although his army was a demonstration of his power, it was also a sign of his weakness. If he could force battle on the Scots – and win – he could expect to force them to a negotiated settlement, but if he failed to engage them, all the propaganda in the world about the cowardly nature of the Scots in refusing battle would not hide the fact that he had failed, despite great effort and expense, to overpower a smaller and weaker neighbour. Evidence that it was possible to defeat the English might have very severe repercussions in Ireland and Wales, particularly in those areas only recently annexed by King Edward, and it would do no good to the prestige of his kingship at home, at a time when there was already serious discontent over taxation, requisitions and increasing demands for military service.

The picture was less bleak for Wallace, insofar as he could hope to win a victory of sorts without actually committing to battle at all. If he could confront Edward but not fight, Edward would eventually have to leave Scotland and disband his army. That might not do a great deal of good for the political career prospects of William Wallace, but it would not do them any harm. The longer he could maintain his position of prominence, the more entrenched he would be in his authority, as people became increasingly accustomed to having a very junior member of the political class as the head of government.

There is no evidence to indicate that Wallace had any intention of actually confronting Edward across the battlefield. No one could have been more intimately aware of the shortcomings of the Scottish army than Wallace himself. As far as we know, William Wallace only ever witnessed two battles, Stirling Bridge and Falkirk, but he must have been aware of the disparity between Edward's force and his own. Frightening the county communities of northern

England was well within the capabilities of the Scottish army, but they were not very well provided with men-at-arms and archers. The only realistic plan for Wallace to adopt was one of avoiding combat with the English army, waiting for it to start breaking up and harassing it on its return journey to England. If he could achieve this he would be able to preserve the army, the basis of his political power, and retain the Guardianship, at least until the next crisis. If Edward could be induced to leave Scotland without making any mark on the political situation, the remaining English garrisons would probably become compromised. The men serving in the garrisons would become less confident of eventual victory, or even of being relieved in the event of a siege, and the credibility of the administration as a whole would be undermined. If at all possible, Edward wanted to take the combat option; Wallace surely did not.

Wallace was nearly successful in his aim. Edward was becoming concerned that the Scots would slip away from him, when he was brought news at Kirkliston. Wallace was on the south side of the River Forth, near Falkirk, a distance of about 8–10km. His army was deployed for battle in four (David Penman, *The Scottish Civil War,* suggests three) circular formations, with archers dispersed around them and a small body of men-at-arms drawn up in the rear. If Edward could close with the Scots quickly enough he might be able to force battle on them, if not in a place of his own choosing exactly, certainly not in theirs.

Large armies of spearmen had secured victories in the past, and would do so again, but only when they could give battle on terms that suited them – constricted battlefields, firm, level ground for the attack or elevated ground for the defence, and a viable response to archery. A more conventional army, one with a greater strength in men-at-arms and archers, was a more versatile beast by far. Its practice could be adapted to suit different conditions with relative ease and efficiency. The move to Falkirk would take the army all day, but it was not a great deal to ask; failing any unexpected developments Edward could reasonably hope to have all of his army gathered under his command in the vicinity of the enemy by the end of the day, with a view to locating him and bringing him to battle the following morning. In this he was entirely successful.

By mid-morning the Scots had been located on a hillside, probably overlooking the Westquarter burn. The position was a strong one, but not particularly so. To the front of the army was the burn, which passed through a boggy area. This had been dismissed as a factor of the Scottish position; however, it would, at the very least, slow down and probably disrupt any general advance by the English army if it deployed from the Linlithgow–Falkirk road. It would seem that Edward had gained a march on the Scots. With Edward's powerful cavalry force on hand, Wallace could hardly expect to extricate his army without interruption. His army would be extremely vulnerable in anything other than carefully selected circumstances, so he really had little choice other than to fight.

The leading cavalry formation, under the Earl of Lincoln, possibly supported by the Earl of Surrey, approached the Scottish right flank with the Falkirk road to their left, where they encountered a marshy area around the Glen burn, forcing them toward the right. The cavalry formations of the king and the bishop of Durham moved on the left of the Scottish army, crossing the upper reach of the Westquarter burn and meeting stiff resistance. Neither attack could make much impression on the Scots; however, horses can be persuaded to do many things, but not to throw themselves bodily into hedges of spears. The solution to the problem lay at hand. Edward committed his archers to the fight and the dense Scottish schiltroms was decided.

The Scottish archers, greatly outnumbered, could offer no worthwhile resistance to their English counterparts. Many were killed and the rest left the field; the Scottish cavalry having already done so. A lot has been written about the abject failure of the nobles to engage, but it is difficult to see what sort of contribution they could have made. Even when the Scots were not divided among themselves, or at least no more so than was normal in a medieval country, they would have struggled to ever put a force of anything like 2,000 men-at-arms in the field. The Falkirk army was not, in any case, a conventional 'national' army raised for a great battle, but a force held in being to confront the enemy until he decided to retire. Also, the country was not united; a significant part of the political community, from whom most men-at-arms were drawn, was in the peace of Edward I, and a considerable portion of the remainder were prisoners of war in England. The Scottish cavalry force at Falkirk probably did not exceed 200 and was therefore in no position to inflict a serious blow on the English cavalry. On the other hand, if the English cavalry brought them to battle, the Scots would assuredly be completely destroyed. The withdrawal of the Scottish cavalry may not have been glorious, but it was the only sensible course to pursue.

The Scottish nobles were not alone in abandoning the fight. Seeing that the battle was lost, William Wallace and his immediate companions fled the field; there was really very little else they could do, other than find a pointless death in a battle where more than enough Scottish people were going to die anyway. As ever, contemporary estimates of casualties are of little value, but there had been a hard business for both sides. Little evidence survives to give any suggestion of casualties. Horse valuation rolls show that more than 100 horses lost in the campaign had to be accounted for. Not all of these claims would actually result in a payment from the Crown – the king might provide a man with a horse in order to have his services. Thomas Lillok, a Roxburghshire man,[16] lost a charger that had been lent to him 'of the king's grace'. Thomas had served King Edward in 1296 as the *socius* of Sir Richard de Horsburgh, and would therefore probably be known to someone in the king's household who could help procure a position for him in the king's household cavalry. However, he may have been serving for his lands in Roxburghshire and have been obliged to borrow a charger from the king's stable so that the king could avail himself of his services.

For Edward, Falkirk was a fine victory over his Scottish enemies. For Wallace, it was the end of his career as a senior political figure. His assumption of leadership had been the product of military success and his loss of it a consequence of military defeat. If he was no longer acceptable to the traditional political and military leadership of Scotland, we should not assume that he had retained his popularity with the people as a whole. It is reasonable to assume that Scottish casualties at Falkirk had been heavy, which can scarcely have endeared Wallace to the community. By imposing his rule, he had raised a great war against the English which may have been very popular indeed in the aftermath of Stirling, but perhaps much less so in the days after Falkirk.

William Wallace resigned the Guardianship by his own choice, or so Fordoun and Bower tell us, on the banks of the Forth shortly after the battle, but there was little else he could do. If he was no longer an asset for recruitment and no longer had the confidence of the rank and file of whatever was left of the army, it was time for him to step aside, even if the magnates had not obliged him to do so, which they undoubtedly would have done.

Victory at Falkirk had immediate benefits for Edward I. He had inflicted a significant defeat on the Scots and had undermined the credibility of William Wallace, but it did not change the course of the war, and, having procured a victory, what exactly was he to do next? Several of his senior 'in capite' tenants had served throughout the campaign without wages and were keen to return to their homes and estates. The financial situation was, in any case, more than just difficult. Edward could hardly find the money needed for the men who had enlisted for pay in the first place, let alone offer wages in the hope of retaining those who had served as volunteers.

For a fortnight he stayed at the Dominican priory at Stirling, recuperating from a kick he had received from his horse on the eve of the battle, before moving to Edinburgh and then making his way across the county to Ayr in search of Robert Bruce. Bruce, unlike his companions in the 'noble revolt', had not adhered to the terms of Edward's peace after the Irvine negotiations, despite promises – unfulfilled – that he would surrender his daughter, Marjory, as a hostage for his future good behaviour. Edward was able to take Lochmaben Castle, but a contemplated operation into Galloway had to be abandoned because of a shortage of manpower.[17]

Edward returned to England before the end of the year. His prestige as king had been enhanced by a signal victory on the battlefield, but he had failed to make any real political progress. Some of the Scottish nobility had entered his peace, but not enough to indicate a general shift in Scottish attitudes, and, as the Lanercost chronicler put it, wherever the bodies of the Scottish lords might be, their hearts were 'with their own people'.

The resignation of Wallace could certainly be seen as a positive outcome from Edward's viewpoint, though even that may not have been as significant as historians have tended to believe. When Wallace assumed or received the office of Guardian in the summer of 1297, the traditional political leaders in Scottish society were either powerless to intervene or were prepared to accept his leadership. Several were of course prisoners of war and therefore had a very limited influence anyway, but it seems much more probable than not that Wallace had effectively been endorsed by the nobles of the Balliol party. By the late summer of 1298 the situation had altered considerably. A number of the men who had been prisoners of war or who had been obliged to perform military service for Edward in Flanders in 1297 had now achieved their release and were, not surprisingly, anxious to re-establish themselves in the political arena.[18] It would be uncharitable to suggest that men like John Comyn, Lord of Badenoch, John Comyn, Earl of Buchan and Robert Bruce, Earl of Carrick spent the summer of 1298 waiting for Wallace to meet a disaster, but they were certainly ready to step into his shoes when the opportunity arose.

The willingness of the Lord of Badenoch and the Earl of Carrick to take up where William Wallace left off is a strong indication that Edward had not really had a successful campaign in 1298. If the Scottish cause had seemed hopeless to them, there would have been little point in accepting the appointment. The Bruce and

Comyn families were the two most significant elements of the Balliol party. The Comyns had come to prominence through a long tradition of service to Scottish kings,[19] and their rise to a position of extensive political influence was based on Crown patronage, so it would have been no surprise that they favoured the continuation of an independent Scottish monarchy. Robert Bruce's decision to join the Balliol party as a Guardian of the realm on behalf of King John was a more complicated matter. If the Balliol party was successful against the English, King John would be restored, a prospect that was highly desirable from a Comyn perspective but obviously rather less so from that of Robert Bruce. It was no secret that Robert had ambitions for the crown, so why should he support the Balliol cause? Naturally the Bruce cause would have been rather closer to his heart, but Robert could not afford to have the political entity of Scotland disappear into the domains of Edward I. If Edward could successfully impose his rule in Scotland for any length of time, the sympathies of the Scottish populace might veer away from the cause of independence toward the cause of peace and stability. If Robert was ever to become king he would need to ensure that Scottish nationhood had not become a thing of the past.

Seal of King Alexander III of Scotland. (Courtesy Michael Penman)

Scottish towns and cities, *c*. 1300.

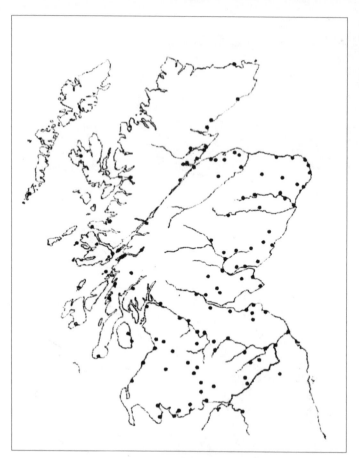

Scottish castles and fortresses. (Author's Collection)

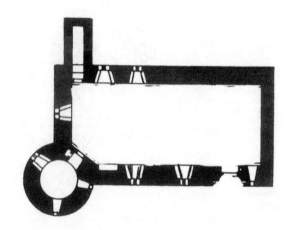

Rait Hall house plan. (After S. Cruden)

Dirleton Castle plan.
(After S. Cruden)

Scalacronica by Sir Thomas Grey of Northumberland.

The Wallace Monument. (Author's Collection)

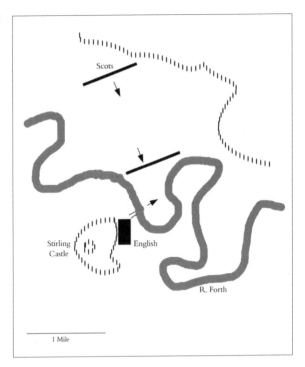

Sketch map of the battle of Stirling Bridge. (Author's Collection)

Scots

Stirling Castle

English

R. Forth

1 Mile

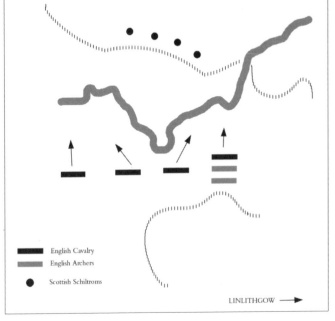

English Cavalry

English Archers

Scottish Schiltroms

LINLITHGOW →

Sketch map of the battle of Falkirk. (Author's Collection)

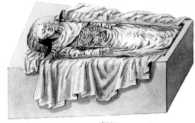

An eighteenth-century illustration of Edward I's body when his tomb was opened in 1774. (*Gothic Eye*)

The enforced deposition of John I (John Balliol) in 1296 from a sixteenth-century Scottish armorial.

Stone grave effigy of a soldier from the west of Scotland wearing a bacinet helmet.

The arms of Edward I showing the three 'leopards of Anjou' that were the traditional symbol of English kingship.

A particularly ornate example of a stone grave effigy.

A Scottish man-at-arms of the thirteenth/
fourteenth century.

A bearded Scottish soldier.

A sixteenth-century depiction of Robert I and his
queen, Elizabeth de Burgh.

The great seal of Robert I.

7

EXILE AND DEFIANCE

Wallace left Scotland at some point in the late summer or autumn of 1299. His defeat at Falkirk had undermined him militarily and politically; for the foreseeable future he had no major contribution to make to the Balliol cause in Scotland, and may even have been regarded as more of a liability than an asset. On the other hand, he could not be ignored or disparaged since to do so would give another propaganda coup to Edward I. There was nothing for him to do in Scotland other than join the ranks of the men-at-arms. If he happened to be killed in action he would join the roll of dead Scottish heroes and be a glorious figure in death, but if he was captured who could know what the English might be able to make of the situation?

Leaving the country was a sensible option, so Wallace made his way to France. What exactly he achieved, or hoped to achieve, during his sojourn in France is difficult to say. Enthusiastic biographers have suggested that he was active in diplomatic affairs, that he served Philip IV as a soldier, that he spent his time with Duns Scotus, a prominent Scottish scholar living in Paris. One possibility that does not seem to have been considered is that Wallace was in France because he had made Scotland too hot to hold him. The new Guardians, John Comyn and Robert Bruce, probably felt that they could manage without having Wallace in the background; with his credibility as a military leader destroyed, there was little Wallace could offer other than his personal service as a man-at-arms. It is unlikely that he had anything much to offer the Scottish diplomatic effort. He may well have been an educated man in the sense of being literate, numerate and having a reasonable knowledge of Latin if, as Blind Harry tells us, he was preparing for the priesthood, but he had no experience of the ways and means of international diplomacy.

As far as we are aware, he had had no experience of soldiering before 1297 either but made a good fist of it, so it could be argued that he might have learned about making diplomatic offensives as he had military ones, but the argument is not sustainable. It is conceivable that he had seen service in the Welsh wars of Edward I, though surely someone would have noticed such a gift to English propaganda. Even if he had seen service, it would be exceedingly unlikely that he would have been party to the command processes of the army unless he had been a person of some stature socially and politically, in which case he would have been a 'weel-kent' (well-known) face to plenty of English soldiers of the 1290s – medieval armies were quite small affairs.

It is also possible that he served in the retinue of a major Scottish noble as a man-at-arms – indeed, it is more likely than not that he would have done so at some point in his upbringing – but, again, that would hardly have made him accustomed to command. It is clear that baronial war was not a normal part of medieval Scottish society; there had been no 'national' or 'kingly' war waged by Scots for a generation, and what there had been – the annexation of the kingdom of Man – was scarcely a major military event.

Peacetime soldiering is a very different business from wartime soldiering and it is a commonplace of history that men – and occasionally women – come to sudden prominence in wartime through a particular gift or have it thrust upon them by circumstances. Since the requirements of peacetime and wartime soldiering are so radically different, it is impossible to know which of the senior officers of an army will actually make good field commanders in the event of war. Wallace's military, and therefore also his political, career was founded on his personal ability – the skills and strength of a big man with a sword. By attracting an increasingly large following of similar men, he was effectively promoting himself in military rank through recruitment. Men joining his band of adherents were looking to receive leadership, not to exert it, so he would have faced little competition for authority as long as he was successful militarily.

The diplomatic world did not offer that sort of opportunity. By the time Wallace arrived in Paris, the Scottish diplomatic 'team' of Baldred Bisset, William of Eaglesham and William Frere, Archdeacon of Lothian, had developed its own policies and practices, it was *au fait* with the procedures and traditions of the European political arena.[1] There was no role for Wallace to perform, other than perhaps that of a heroic figure who could be shown to the French as an example of Scottish determination and chivalry. The problem with that, of course, was that sooner or later everyone of any importance in Paris would have seen or met with William Wallace and started to question his importance. If he was such a fine soldier and man-at-arms, what was he doing in France? Why was he not fighting in Scotland?

After Falkirk, the Guardianship had passed to Sir John Comyn of Badenoch and Robert Bruce, Earl of Carrick,[2] but theirs was a difficult relationship, to say the least. In August 1299 they had been conducting operations from Selkirk forest when a fight erupted between them during a council meeting at Peebles. The report of an English agent received by Sir Robert Hastang, the Plantagenet sheriff of Roxburgh, and therefore Edward's chief military officer in the vicinity, shows the tension in the Scottish camp and is worth quoting in its entirety:

At the council Sir David Graham demanded the lands and goods of Sir William Wallace because he was leaving the kingdom without the permission of the guardians. And Sir Malcolm Wallace, Sir William's brother, answered that neither his lands or goods should be given away, for they were protected by the peace in which Wallace had left the kingdom, since he was leaving to work for the good of kingdom. At this the two knights gave the lie to each other and drew their daggers. And since Sir David Graham was of Sir John Comyn's following and Sir Malcolm Wallace of the earl of Carrick's following it was reported to the earl of Buchan and John Comyn that a fight had broken out without their knowing it; and John Comyn leaped at the earl of Carrick and seized him by the throat, and the earl of Buchan turned on the bishop of St Andrews, declaring that treason and lèse-majesté were being plotted. Eventually the Steward and others came between them and quietened them down. At that moment a letter was brought from beyond the Firth of Forth, telling how Sir Alexander Comyn and Lachlan were burning and devastating the district they were in, attacking the people of Scotland. So it was ordained then that the bishop of St Andrews should have all the castles in his hands as principal guardian, and the earl of Carrick and John Comyn be with him as joint-guardians of the kingdom. And that same Wednesday, after the letter had been read, they all left Peebles.[3]

Evidently Wallace was still in Scotland in the summer of 1299, but was no longer at the centre of political or military decision-making. We should not assume that he was not active personally, but it seems that he was not at Peebles with the main body of the Scots. His departure was evidently imminent, however, hence the claims of Sir David Graham. Graham's attack on William Wallace may be an indication of the level to which the former Guardian's prestige had sunk. If Wallace had still been a popular heroic figure it would have been rash indeed for Graham to make a move on Wallace's lands and goods. It is of course possible that there was a perception that Wallace had done very nicely personally out of the Guardianship and that Graham was articulating a resentment shared by others. As a younger son, possibly a third son, Wallace would have had little prospect of acquiring land of his own that he could pass on to a son 'in heritage'. Any portion of the family estate that came into Wallace's hands would be much more likely than not to be a life interest that would return to the main body of the estate on his death.[4]

Graham's claim was surely motivated by the political agenda of his patron, Sir John Comyn, or was at least acceptable to Comyn, but attacking Wallace would have been a risky undertaking. Even if the former Guardian had become so unpopular that a move to acquire his property was unlikely to be opposed among the nobility or by the wider community, he was still a force to be reckoned with on a personal level. Graham might be able to procure a political decision in his favour, but that would not prevent William Wallace from killing him.

How Wallace spent his time in exile is a matter of debate. He certainly received a letter of credence from Philip IV, in which the king asked his officers at the curia to give whatever help they could to his dear and trusted knight, William Wallace of Scotland. Whether he actually managed to arrange an audience with the Pope is not known, though he obviously would have had little to discuss other than the political condition of Scotland. It has been suggested that he would have met with John Balliol, who was released to papal custody in 1299, but there is no evidence that he did so.

By 1303 Wallace was back in Scotland, possibly at the request of William Lamberton, but not in the capacity of a significant leader. The war had continued in his absence, and the Scots had enjoyed a deal of success. No great victories had been won, but there again no great defeats had been inflicted in the period 1299–1302. The military situation had not stabilised, insofar as the Scots could neither prevent nor even confront major English armies, but the gains made by Edward's expeditions tended to be lost to the Scots once the army was dismissed.

Edward was making progress. He was able to arrange for the construction of 'peles' at Selkirk and Linlithgow,[5] and was endeavouring to make another at Dunfermline. These 'peles' were not castles, but army establishments. Their function was to provide a number of centres of operation for mobile columns of men-at-arms who could impose Edward's rule throughout the vicinity. The forces of his 'permanent' administration were not up to the task of extending his rule throughout the country, but the Scots were incapable of dislodging them. The absence of battles of great stature did not mean the presence of peace. The nature of the war was largely a business of demonstrating local superiority in order to be able to exert lordship, and was almost exclusively conducted by small parties of men-at-arms, a milieu in which William Wallace would have been perfectly at home, and which he doubtless joined on his return from France.

The Guardians had not been able to expel the English from the whole country, but they certainly had more control over more of Scotland more of the time than the Plantagenets. The vital castle of Stirling had been recovered after the Battle of Stirling Bridge and remained in Scottish hands until after the Strathord agreement of 1304. The economy was functioning, sheriffs and judges carried out their normal duties and the war was being conducted in an effective, if unadventurous, way.[6] The course of events during the absence of Wallace had proven that he was not indispensable to the Balliol party: the former Guardian was now just one of many men-at-arms and knights serving the cause of King John.

The loss of the Guardianship, and perhaps his prolonged absence overseas, undoubtedly took the shine off Wallace's reputation to some degree, but he was still probably capable of attracting the adherence of men of a similar station and outlook, if only on the basis of his personal prowess as a fighter – which was, of course, the foundation of his rise to power in the first place. He was no longer a senior figure in the command structure, but he does seem to have had a following of his own and to have been active against the English, though not, perhaps, really under the command of the Balliol party. He does not appear to have been involved in their operations to any great extent, though that may be more a reflection of the survival of record material than of the level and intensity of his activity. He was not, for example, present at the Battle of Roslin in February 1303, though it was precisely the sort of action where the Scots had most need of men of his status, but he was in action against a substantial force under Sir Aymer de Valence at Earnside in September 1304.[7]

By this time, however, the political situation had changed radically. In July 1302 the French had been badly beaten by the Flemings at Courtrai, and Philip IV had been obliged to make peace with Edward. Until this point Philip had been able to insist on the inclusion of the Scots in any truce arrangements: Philip's weakness was Edward's opportunity. He was at last able to have peace with France without abstaining from war in Scotland. The Scots had struggled to contain Edward when he was at war with the French; they had little chance of defeating him unaided, and in February 1304 the Balliol party came to terms with Edward's representatives at Strathord.[8] The relatively lenient terms allowed to the Scots in general did not extend to certain specified individuals. William Wallace, no longer referred to as a knight, was carefully excluded. No man was to accept him into Edward's peace on any terms other than unconditional surrender.[9]

Part of the price the nobles of the Balliol party paid for acceptance into Edward's peace was, naturally, the acceptance of an obligation to uphold the law and to persecute the enemies of the king.[10] Wallace was not the only man to have been excluded from the Strathord agreement, but he was certainly one of Edward's most urgent priorities. Quite why Wallace chose to remain in Scotland at this juncture is something of a mystery. A man of his evident talents as a combatant would have been able to find reasonably lucrative employment overseas. While patriotic fervour was surely part of his motivation, he may have felt, and probably correctly, that he would not be able to have a secure future wherever he went. Edward was obviously bent on procuring Wallace for trial if he possibly could, but there is no reason to assume that he would not have settled for his murder if all else failed.

The capture of Sir William Wallace at Glasgow in 1305 by Sir John Menteith can hardly have come as a surprise to anyone, including, perhaps especially, Wallace himself. Although he must still have been able to motivate men and women to assist him in his struggle, once the Balliol party had made their peace at Strathord, Wallace must have been aware that his days were numbered. The men who had served the Balliol cause – nobles, burgesses, clerics and commoners – were now in the enemy camp and were obliged to do everything in their power to bring an end to Wallace's operations. From the moment King John accepted Philip IV's change in his policy toward Scotland (though he probably had no choice in the matter and little interest in recovering his kingdom anyway), the Balliol cause was finally and fatally compromised. The Scots could not rationally continue a war to restore the king if the king did not want to return to Scotland.

Edward I's administration was beginning to achieve effective lordship in an increasingly large portion of the country, and the people were exhausted. Wallace and men like him – there were probably others who, for whatever reason, had been effectively excluded from the peace agreement – were not an effective source of authority or a realistic focus for recruitment. In the summer of 1297 Wallace had been able to raise men in large numbers relatively easily, initially through his personal abilities as a man-at-arms and a leader, later by virtue of the fact that he had enjoyed some success in battle. An important factor in the recruitment of Wallace's army in July and August 1297 was the fact that it existed at all; it provided a vehicle for political – which under the circumstances almost inevitably meant military – activity. At some point that summer, William Wallace's force made a transition. It ceased to be a retinue of men-at-arms making attacks of opportunity on isolated elements of the occupation and started to become, by medieval standards, a large army with much more sophisticated needs. It also became a political institution, one made for the purpose of liberating the country from the Plantagenet occupation; as such, it was a focus for men who were willing to fight.

By the late summer of 1305 there was no Scottish army, just the odd handful of men who would not or could not be reconciled to the Edwardian rule that now extended to their fellow Scots. Whatever sympathy there may have been for William Wallace in the political community or in the society of Scotland generally, there must have been many who felt that 'enough was enough' and that it was long past time the business was settled. The Balliol cause was discredited, thousands of people had been killed, ruined and imprisoned and the economy was deeply damaged.

Furthermore, Wallace had a price on his head. There would be rewards for the person who captured Wallace, but there would also very likely be sharp treatment for anyone who sheltered him. Wallace's standing in the wider community of Scots may not have been quite as healthy as the chroniclers and historians suggest. His period of personal rule had come to an end after the Battle of Falkirk. The chroniclers Fordoun and Bower and the poet Blind

Harry all blame the treachery of the Comyns and/or Robert Bruce for the Falkirk disaster, but at the time Wallace must have carried the responsibility in the eyes of most people since he was the commanding officer. Scottish chronicle writers of the later fourteenth and fifteenth centuries had something of a shared agenda: animosity to English expansionism and the glorification of heroes long dead. There was no mileage for them in telling readers anything that might throw any doubt on the esteem of the common people of Scotland for William Wallace, but after Falkirk his name may not have been a good advertisement for the Balliol cause.

Wallace's survival in Scotland from the Strathord agreement until his eventual capture does indicate that he was either still well thought of by a substantial part of the community, who were willing to risk life and limb to support him, or that he had sufficient military strength in his following to demand whatever he needed. Had he been entirely reliant on violence to provision his men and horses, his remaining popularity would have evaporated quickly and English propagandists would have been quick to recount his depredations, but it is most probable that he drew aid both from the willing and the unwilling. Increasingly, however, his position was untenable. He could no longer attract large numbers of men to his banner, and even if he did, what was he going to do with them?

In 1297 he had enjoyed enough support in the political community to allow him to assume the Guardianship. The recovery of the Scottish administration in 1297 was not the work of William Wallace alone; if anything, it is possible that Wallace, as a proven leader, was as much adopted as accepted by those members of the Balliol party of the Scottish political community as were at liberty. Without the support of the political community, there would have been no Scottish administration to carry on the business of governing the country, thereby allowing Wallace to get on with the war. In 1304 that community had accepted the lordship of Edward I and as Edward's officers and prominent figures in society, they had an obligation to capture Wallace, and it was inevitable that they should do so. In August 1305 Wallace was captured by Sir John Menteith at Glasgow, and was sent south to face trial.

William Wallace's trial was never intended to be a demonstration of justice, just the recitation of a formal litany of charges presumed to be true by the fact that they had been made. There was no question of a defence. There was no defence Wallace could make that would change the outcome of the trial, but it would have been redundant anyway, in the sense that to defend his position would be a recognition of Edward I's right to hold him for trial at all. Wallace was accused of treason, but he had never given his allegiance to King Edward and had fought him tooth and nail as the aggressive invader that he most certainly was. The point of the trial was not to assess the guilt of William Wallace, but to demonstrate the power and majesty of Edward I, to show clearly the Scottish war was at an end, to show what happened to people who resisted his kingship, to give a symbol of vengeance achieved to the subjects of England and to provide a great entertainment for the citizens of London.

Executions continued to be a public spectacle until well into the nineteenth century. Indeed, their removal from public view was more a matter of the changing tastes of the ruling class than of any apathy on the part of the community. Hangings were relatively commonplace, though by no means a daily occurrence, but ritualistic killings and dismemberings were a great rarity and were welcomed as spectacular entertainments. William Wallace made the journey to the scaffold dragged on a hurdle behind a horse for about 6km around the City of London. It would have been a slow business, unlikely to have taken less than two hours and very probably much longer, since the streets would have been crowded by Londoners keen to see a rare spectacle. Considerable damage could be inflicted on the body by drawing it through the streets, and it would seem that it was not uncommon for the accused to be wrapped in hide, to protect them sufficiently to ensure that they would still be alive when they reached their destination.

Dragged from Westminster to the Tower, then to Aldgate and finally to Smithfield, Wallace was given to executioners to hang by the neck, but not until death. While he still lived he was cut down, and, still conscious, had his torso split open so that his organs could be removed and burnt on a brazier in front of him. At length – and the fame of the executioner rested on his ability to make the death of the victim slow as well as agonising – his head was removed for display on London Bridge and the four quarters of his body sent to Newcastle, Berwick, Perth and Stirling – a trophy for the people of Northumberland after their sufferings at the hands of William Wallace, and a warning to the inhabitants of Berwick, Stirling and Perth.

Edward's determination to ensure the complete destruction of William Wallace must have been apparent at the time, and it is worth giving some thought as to why the king of England, having successfully brought the Scots into his peace, should have been so relentless in his pursuit of a man who, though he had been of great stature at one time, was now 'yesterday's man'. For reasons of personal prestige, it was important that someone should be seen to pay a dire penalty for the trouble to which the king of England had been put. A failure to ensure that the people were aware that he had utterly suppressed the Scots might be construed as weakness, or at least lead to resentment that the cost in blood and money that the English had borne in Scotland had not resulted in a clear victory.

In order to procure a settlement in February 1304, Edward had had to offer very lenient terms to the Balliol party, largely because he had come to the conclusion that he could not secure Scotland without the acceptance and active support of the political community. Had he seized and executed one or more of the Balliol party leaders – the Earl of Buchan for example – he would have compromised any prospect of gaining the confidence of the rest of the nobility. He might have liked very much to have taken action against several of them, but not if he wanted to reach an early settlement. The Scots had effectively been abandoned by their own king, but they were not finished militarily and it might yet be a major struggle to overcome them. If Edward was to have peace without waging more campaigns that he could not really afford, he would have to pay a price; he would have to settle for Wallace as the focus of his vengeance.

Edward not only wanted peace, he wanted it in a hurry. He was no longer a young man, nor so hale as he had been in the past, and would have been eager to see his projects completed before he died. If he could manage to make his rule acceptable in Scotland he would have extended the scope of the kingship he had inherited, a very natu-ral ambition for a medieval monarch, and he wanted men to think well of him when he was dead. If Scotland was at peace and under his rule when he died – an event that could not be many years distant – he would have been a 'success' within his own frame of reference. Even if his son were to 'lose' Scotland in the future, the loss would reflect on his failure to maintain Edward's legacy, not Edward's failure to provide a secure and stable patrimony.

The men who joined Edward's peace do not seem to have been particularly committed to the capture of Wallace, given that he remained at large for nearly eighteen months, but some of them at least were probably not unhappy to hear of his demise. If the Strathord agreement was to be effective, men like Wallace would have to curb their enthusiasm for the Balliol cause. If it was to be a temporary expedient, a lull in the hostilities rather than a final accord, the activities of Wallace would be less than desirable. As long as they kept fighting, Edward would maintain garrisons in Scotland capable of mounting operations and imposing his government. Like the 'Real' and 'Continuity' IRA splinter groups of recent years, Wallace, and men like him, may have been seen as an obstacle to progress, even by the most sympathetic observers. William had provided leadership for the Scottish cause for a critical period in 1297–98 and had doubtless served his prince assiduously thereafter, but his capture may have come as something of a relief to the people of Scotland in 1305.

8

BUT WHAT WAS IT ALL *FOR*?

Never one to miss an opportunity, Edward I was able to manipulate the various claimants to the Scottish crown in the Great Cause of 1291–92 into accepting him as their feudal superior. Over the following three years, he goaded the successful candidate, King John I, into 'rebellion' through consistently undermining the authority and therefore the prestige and credibility of his kingship by hearing appeals from John's courts and eventually, in 1295, demanding military service from King John and a number of Scottish magnates for his campaign against the French. King John made his defiance to Edward, repudiating his acceptance of Edward as liege lord on the grounds that it had been given under duress and that Edward was acting beyond the bounds of reasonable behaviour.

Conscious that they could not readily withstand Edward on their own, the Scots needed to find allies and formed an offensive and defensive alliance with the French. None of this impressed Edward in the slightest and he invaded Scotland in April 1296, destroyed the Scottish cavalry in battle at Dunbar, deposed John, took the allegiance of a great swathe of Scottish noble, clerical and commercial society, led his troops as far north as Elgin, installed his own administration and made his way to Berwick, where he called a Parliament at the end of August.

His remarkable progress through the east of Scotland that summer was a *tour de force* of conventional military practice. Towns and castles surrendered on his arrival and there was no sign of resistance on the part of the Scots when Edward returned to his other affairs in England and on the continent, leaving several small garrisons to secure his occupation. If he assumed that he had dealt with Scotland, he was much mistaken. Within the year he faced the opposition of a Scottish administration which soon controlled virtually all of Scotland north of the river Tay and was making steady progress in reducing English power through the rest of the country.

The extent to which the entire period between 1286 and 1307 is seen as little more than a backdrop to the careers of Scotland's most cherished heroes – William Wallace and Robert Bruce – is proof positive of the remarkable success of Bruce propaganda,[1] constructed both in his own lifetime and in the works of Barbour, Fordoun, Wyntoun and Bower in the following century and a half. They, and their successors right down to the twentieth century, tended to portray the efforts of the Scots in resisting Edward I as a vehicle for the heroism and martyrdom of Wallace and a delaying action to keep the English at bay until the right circumstances developed for Robert Bruce to seize the throne just a few months after Wallace's betrayal, capture, trial and execution.

We can be confident that the situation was not seen in that light by the participants in and supporters of the various Guardianships[2] which endeavoured to maintain Scotland's status as a sovereign country with a sovereign lord, King

John – even if he was a captive in a foreign land. In theory, and certainly in practice during the early years of the conflict, the Guardian administrations were committed to the restoration of the Balliol line rather than the recovery of Scottish independence by any means, although the latter stages of the conflict were perhaps more a question of holding out for good terms of surrender. Had Edward wished to do so, he could have restored John to the Scottish throne at any time, on the same basis as John's previous kingship.

The extent to which that could be considered 'independence' is perhaps open to question from a twenty-first century perspective, although, having been deposed once already, it would not be surprising if John refused to be reinstated. He apparently made a deposition to an English notary public to the effect that he had encountered nothing but trouble among the Scots, and intimated that he had no desire to have anything much to do with them in the future. John's refusal would have utterly compromised the position of those fighting the Plantagenet occupation – they would have had no cause to fight for.

If a Balliol restoration was a course of action Edward ever considered there is no record of it, and the Scots continued to fight in the name of King John, though to what extent the conflict developed into a war of national identity, and how quickly, is impossible to say. It is clear that by 1304 at the latest some men were quite prepared to carry on the king's fight even without a king to fight for, but that does not mean that they would be willing to do so forever. Although medieval monarchs were, in many ways, rather closer to their subjects than modern ones, they were seen as the ultimate source of authority and enjoyed a certain amount of awe that would be denied a mere officer of state, even one so exalted as a Guardian of the Realm.

The Guardians exercised the power of the king, but with the authority of the Community of the Realm, or at least with the assent of the political community.[3] With the sole exception of William Wallace, all of the men who served as Guardians for John I's kingship were men of great standing in their communities and of some prominence nationally. The most junior of them, other than Wallace, was Andrew Murray, a man of baronial rank, of considerable wealth and very well connected throughout the noble community of the north, particularly to the Comyn family.

The Scots had some experience of non-regal government. During the reign of Margaret of Norway, throughout the Great Cause, and possibly in the reign of John Balliol himself, Scotland had been ruled by Guardians.[4] These Guardians were drawn from the uppermost ranks of what medieval society perceived as the most valid representation of the Scottish people, the Community of the Realm.[5] With the exception of Murray and Wallace all of the Guardians were magnates, whether temporal or ecclesiastical; they were men accustomed to wielding authority in their own sphere of power and had been entrusted with regal powers by their peers; they could be just as easily undermined as supported by noble interest groups and were therefore vulnerable to threats of disobedience, defiance or even defection if they offended other members of the aristocracy.

By the standards of medieval political structures, the willingness of the Scots to accept non-regal government, particularly the willingness to accept government by committee on behalf of a minor, and a female minor at that, indicates a remarkably sophisticated political consciousness and confidence. The Community of the Realm was the practical expression of the 'political identity or nationhood'[6] of the Scots over and above the institution of monarchy.

1 Cambuskenneth Abbey. (Author's Collection)

2 Torphichen Receptory. (Author's Collection)

3 Edinburgh Castle from Arthur's Seat. (Author's Collection)

4 Dirleton Castle. (Author's Collection)

5 An arming jacket. (Author's Collection)

6 A mounted man-at-arms. (Author's Collection)

7 A spearman. (Author's Collection)

8 Schiltron. (Author's Collection)

9 A polearm. (Author's Collection)

10 John I. (Author's Collection)

11 A hobelar. (Author's Collection).

12 A trebuchet. (Author's Collection)

13 Inchcolm Abbey. (Author's Collection)

14 View of Stirling Bridge battlefield from the north. (Author's Collection)

15 View of Stirling Bridge battlefield from the castle. (Author's Collection)

16 View of River Forth from mid-river. (Author's Collection)

The Community of the Realm may have been dominated by the most powerful alignments of the nobility,
but it represented the 'totality of the King's free subjects'
and 'the political entity in which they and the King were
comprehended'.[7] The practical need to carry on the king's
government when there was, effectively, no king at all was
perfectly understood, and the authority of the Community
of the Realm was seen as adequate for the provision of government during a royal minority or as a forum in which to
address a specific problem, such as a succession dispute, but
it was not considered an adequate permanent substitute for
the personal rule of a monarch. Like any other medieval
monarchy, to make Scotland's government 'complete' it
needed a king, so the primary objective of all the Guardians
(including Robert Bruce) from 1297 to 1304 was to bring
about the restoration of King John.

In order to achieve this, the Guardians would have to
procure his release from English (then papal, then French)
custody,[8] and to do that they would have to establish and
maintain a secure Scottish sovereignty.[9] In order to achieve
administrative credibility at home and diplomatic credibility abroad, the Guardians needed to establish a Scottish
administration in direct competition with that of King
Edward, and the main focus of that administration would
have to be the successful pursuit of the war, leading to the
ejection of the occupation.

The speed with which such a government was erected
would suggest that the views of the Guardians were not at
odds with the sympathies of the population as a whole, and
the Guardians were able to exercise effective power in all
the departments of medieval government – judicial, legisla-
tive, diplomatic and, above all, military – with the authority
conferred on them by the Community of the Realm.

To what extent Wallace had these powers conferred after the Battle of Stirling Bridge and to what extent he simply assumed them is impossible to say. It seems clear that he and Murray had the benefit of a considerable degree of support from the traditional sources of political leadership, and Wallace certainly seems to have had the wholehearted enthusiasm of the army, so it would have taken a very confident person to contest his authority.

If the Scots were fighting for the reinstatement of King John, what were they hoping to achieve if they were successful? The constant themes of the Scots in their negotiations with the English and their petitions to the papacy, other than the return of the king, is the demand for the reintroduction of the laws and customs of John's reign, the acceptance by Edward I of Scottish sovereignty and the removal of English garrisons. The restoration of the king may not have been quite so unlikely a prospect as it might seem; the Scots were remarkably successful in their diplomatic campaigns from 1297, until Philip IV was obliged to abandon his Scottish allies through the defeat of his army at Courtrai, an event that effectively removed Philip's capacity, if not his willingness, to carry on his conflict with Edward. The transfer of King John to the custody of the Pope and then to King Philip of France must have been an encouragement to the Scots generally.

One man for whom it was not good news was Robert Bruce, Earl of Carrick and Lord of Annandale. The restoration of the Balliol line would seriously compromise any prospect of a Bruce succession to the Scottish throne. Bruce might be prepared to fight under the Balliol banner as a vehicle for his own career ambitions, but not if the return of King John was to become a reality: Bruce made his peace with King Edward and joined the occupation.

The defection of Robert to the Plantagenet cause has been a difficult topic for Scottish and English writers. It undermines Robert's patriotic credentials. However, as with most people, Robert's chief priority was himself and his dependants. Bruce may have fought for King John in his absence, but he had not been prepared to turn out for the Balliol cause in the summer of 1296, a choice which he might have cause to regret should John be restored.

Resentment of the occupation generally was undoubtedly a factor encouraging resistance, so it is worth giving some thought to the aspects of King Edward's rule that engendered that resent. The clerical community of Scotland was broadly supportive of the campaign against the English. Part of their interest lay in the unusual relationship between the Scottish Church and the Holy See. As a 'Special Daughter' of the Papacy, Scottish prelates were free of archiepiscopal supervision. If Scotland were to be annexed by England, the Scottish Church would sooner or later be made subject to either Canterbury or York, which would have serious repercussions for their financial position and for their powers of patronage and, of course, their own career prospects.[10]

The nobility faced a similar problem. The distribution of offices under the Crown (and, of course, the ability to influence its wearer) would be adversely affected – in their view – by a change not only in the ruling house but in the actual seat of government. Scottish nobles may not always have been in full accord with their kings, but at least the king was reasonably accessible. The expense of attending the king in London or Winchester would have been enormous, and cutting a dash among the English aristocracy would have been beyond the financial capacity of all but the very richest Scottish nobles.

Like the clergy, the nobility feared the 'intrusion' of outsiders into positions of authority. The networks of lordships and offices through which the great families of Scotland furthered their interests and protected their adherents would be destabilised by the appointment of people with no interest in the domestic politics of the Scots. In a sense, the Wars of Independence could be described as an issue about whether the great and good preferred to be the big fish in a small pond or, relatively, rather less significant fish in a much larger pond. The choice was not a simple one – the assimilation of Scottish kingship into English kingship would certainly mean that access to the king would be more difficult and costly and that there would be greater competition for patronage, but the power and prestige of English kings was very great indeed, and the potential for advancement from English monarchs was very much greater than anything Scottish kings could offer, including the possibility of profitable service overseas.

The noble classes were not alone in their concerns. The gentry, burgesses and wealthier tenants were faced with the likelihood of higher taxes and increased obligations of military service. In practice, very little was demanded in the way of military service[11] beyond customary man-at-arms obligations on the nobility and the more successful members of the mercantile community, and taxes are resented whether they are increased or not, regardless of whose name they are raised in. Whether or not Edward's occupation was very onerous was not necessarily the issue: it was perceived as being more burdensome than the government of Scottish kings had been and it was thought that things would probably get worse rather than better the longer it continued – or at least that was the claim of the Scots in the surrender arrangements of 1304.

The Community of the Realm did not, of course, represent the whole of Scottish society, nor was it intended that it should; it only directly represented those with an obvious stake in the country. The labouring classes may have paid their rents and served in the army, but their views are unrecorded. It is reasonable to assume that, in the main, decisions of allegiance were the province of the landlord classes, but it would be rash to assume that the lord would not take account of the opinions and interests of his subordinates. Further, if called upon, the tenant was obliged to fight under his lord, but he might choose to fight anyway – Wallace was able to raise substantial numbers of troops without the support of the nobility.[12] Given the popularity of Wallace's campaigning, it is not inconceivable that some nobles, in order to show 'good lordship', may have had to support the Guardians against their own inclinations.[13] If Wallace's rising involved a measure of social discontent[14] a wise lord might be obliged to take care to retain the confidence of his people; on the other hand, the lord as an individual might be captured and persuaded or forced to serve Edward and find himself on the opposite side of the battlefield to his tenants.[15]

Alongside the social and personal issues, the Scots fought out of injured pride and xenophobia, and they fought for what they saw as a national interest – there was a widespread sympathy for the concept of national 'liberty', in the sense of political independence, and they fought against 'the kind of intensive government which they were quite unaccustomed to, and which contrasted greatly, with a touch of rose-tinted nostalgia, with life under the King of Scots'.[16] If we acknowledge the consistency with which the Scots seek the restoration of their country's autonomy, and the frequency with which we encounter expressions of and reference to nationality, we must accept nationalism as a force in medieval Scotland[17] and therefore as one of the issues for which the Scots fought between 1297 and 1304.

Traditionally, historians have been less than generous to the leaders of Scottish resistance to Edward, with the exceptions of Murray and Wallace. The early death of Murray made him an impeccable patriot; he did not have time to do anything of a questionable nature (such as changing sides) or to be associated with any disasters. Wallace's death made him a hero, but his power in the Community of the Realm rested solely on his success as a military leader, and he lost his position as Guardian shortly after the defeat at Falkirk.[18] Wallace's term of government lasted for little more than a year and, by the later stages of the war period of 1296–1304, he was no longer in a position to come to terms with the English administration. His successors, John Comyn and Robert Bruce, stand accused of self-interest, duplicity, manipulation and both the threat and the reality of physical violence. It should come as no surprise that all of these criticisms are perfectly valid. If the new Guardians were careful of their interests, we should bear in mind that they did have an awful lot of interests to be careful of and that, without the strength and prestige afforded them by these interests – land, patronage, Crown offices, alliances and allegiances – it would not have been possible for them to govern. Duplicity and manipulation is the very stuff of political life in any society, and the violence of Bruce and Comyn is perhaps shocking, but surely not surprising.

The tension between the two Guardians – Comyn, premier baron in the realm, head of a family with a strong tradition of Crown service,[19] and irreproachably patriotic, and Bruce, whose wholehearted commitment might be questioned, given his regal ambition –was sufficiently strong to make the appointment of a third Guardian necessary. The political community chose Bishop Lamberton, to keep his colleagues from one another's throats. The government of the Guardians was less effective than it might have been because of internal dissent, but Scotland was not always easily governed by kings in peacetime let alone by regencies or guardianships in wartime. If we assume either 'altruism' or 'self-interest' on the part of the Guardians, we assume too much, and must remember that the interests of the great and powerful were not necessarily inimical to those of the society as a whole. Most people, most of the time, prefer peace and stability to any other condition, and the various Guardians were endeavouring to achieve just that. Under the circumstances prevailing in Scotland in 1296–1304, keeping any kind of an administration afloat was quite an achievement in itself.

The factors that brought the Scots to the negotiating table were largely external rather internal. Diplomatic isolation, resulting from the Anglo-French peace agreement of May 1303[20] and in particular the reduced likelihood of King Philip allowing King John to return to Scotland, turned a hard struggle into an impossible task. The position of the Scots was not promising before this turn of events – Edward was able to pay a great deal of attention to the military and political situations in Scotland in 1303–04. His foreign and domestic problems eased sufficiently for him to pass that winter at Linlithgow in Lothian, supervising operations against the Balliol party and preventing them from recovering their position through the winter months, a pattern that had developed over the years since 1296.

By the close of 1303, the inability of the Guardians to provide a king and the physical and economic exhaustion of the country overcame the will of the community to continue the fight. Due to the shortage of documents, it is impossible to develop a clear picture of the Scottish administration, other than to assume that the institutions of the state continued in much the same fashion as they had under King John – otherwise, what indeed were the Scots fighting for?

Regardless of *how* exactly the Scottish government functioned, the fact is that it *did* function. The Guardians were able to exercise the power necessary to call parliaments and councils,[21] collect rents and military service, hold courts and conduct a vigorous diplomatic campaign, while waging war against a vastly better-resourced opponent. Neither the war nor the diplomacy would pay for themselves, so revenue must have been raised, with all that implies for the existence of chancery[22] (the crown's secretariat) and exchequer[23] (the crown's financial administration) and the willingness of the community to accept the authority of these institutions. The only part of the administration that might be expected to support itself from its own income was the judiciary,[24] which could impose fines and confiscations on wrong-doers, which goes some way to explaining the determination of the Scots to speedily provide sheriffs in the counties they recovered, although the use of the sheriff's position as a visible evidence of the power of the government was also an important consideration. As the chief financial, judicial and military officer, whose appointment lay in the hands of the Crown, the sheriff, assuming he could exert his authority effectively, was a useful focus for the sympathetic and a deterrent to the unsympathetic.

The Balliol party maintained their struggle against Edwardian occupation for a period of more than seven years, and though they failed to achieve the restoration of

King John or the political independence of Scotland, they were never overwhelmed by their opposition.

An indication of the success of the Scots can be found in the terms of their eventual surrender. The rather lenient terms that Edward agreed with almost all of the Scots, as individuals and as representatives of their cause, do not suggest an abject surrender, and although Edward's commitment to the laws and customs of King John's reign was obviously open to question, he was not above dealing with problems in his Scottish domain by referring to the practices used in 'the days of the King of Scotland'. The continuation of established practice was not a sop to Scottish sentiments; it was in line with Edward's general policy toward Scotland. He had no great interest in changing the way in which Scotland was governed, only that it should be governed strictly in his own interest. Had he been successful in the conquest of Scotland, then no doubt over the succeeding years Scottish legal, commercial and military practices would have gradually fallen into line with those in England, but that would really be incidental to Edward. What he wanted from Scotland was a secure northern border, money and military service, and the recognition and reality of his kingship throughout the British Isles.

Of course, whether or not the survival of an independent Scottish government should be viewed as an achievement is dependent on a particular point of view. There was nothing particularly more natural or inevitable about the development of a Scottish nation than any other country, and there was nothing inevitable about its surviving Edward's attempt at annexation. The Community of the Realm did not of course represent all Scots. Some were actively engaged against the 'Patriotic' cause, and for a variety of reasons – the search for stability, peer pressure, the fact that one's life and livelihood were in an occupied zone or that one had homage obligations to Edward I. Most importantly, resented or not, the occupation did gain an increasing acceptance in the community, if raising revenue can be taken as a measure of the effectiveness of the government.[25] Such growing acceptance does not necessarily imply intimidation on the part of the English or despair on the part of the Scots; it is more a matter of the Scots adapting to a new order. The nascent nationalism to be found among some Scots was by no means universal; for some, the importance of homage given – even in the rather questionable circumstances of 1296 – was of greater significance, or was at least taken seriously enough to deter casual defections.

Over and above the threats to life, limb and property risked in resisting Edward (and it was obviously rather easier for the people outside the areas held by the occupation administration to be patriotic) it was, as Fiona Watson has pointed out,[26] difficult for people to be sure what constituted the correct ethical response to conflicts of allegiance. Promises extracted under duress could in theory legitimately be repudiated, or allegiance could be refused by the strong-hearted, but either was a risky undertaking in the volatile environment of medieval Scotland. Acceptance of Edward's rule could have very real attractions: for the nobility, who would obtain protection for their life and possessions, for the clerics, who would ensure the security of their appointments, and, potentially, for quite ordinary people like those 'King's husbandmen',[27] who had petitioned King Edward for greater security in their tenancies.

The careers of Malise, Earl of Strathearn and his eldest son (also Malise) clearly show the problems of divided loyalties among the magnates. Malise the elder could reasonably claim that his initial submission to Edward in 1296 was made under duress, but with his two younger sons hostage in England, he can scarcely be said to have had freedom of action. Malise left Edward's peace to support the Guardians after the Battle of Stirling Bridge, by which time his sons had become members of Edward of Caernarvon's court. After the surrender at Irvine he served Edward I and then Edward II faithfully until captured at the fall of Perth, but his son served Robert I throughout his career. He apparently defied his father out of 'purely nationalist sentiment',[28] but the pragmatic value of being assured of having a family member on the winning side was surely obvious to all concerned.

The greatest achievement of the Scots in their kingless years was simply the maintenance of a Scottish kingdom without the supposedly vital component of the king. The Community of the Realm, as represented by the Guardians, acted in what it perceived to be the interests of the country, and the government worked through the traditional agencies of the country. The same offices and officers of state endured in the civil sphere, and although there is very probably a measure of truth in the view that Wallace's early success was based on a 'popular movement with a measure of social discontent in its make-up'[29] the forces employed in support of the Balliol government by MacDougall and Bruce in the west and by Murray in the north[30] were mustered by the 'normal' officers of the Crown, fulfilling their traditional roles as leaders in their local communities.

The ineffectiveness of these forces has as much to do with the generally demilitarised nature of thirteenth-century Scotland as defeat in battle at Dunbar in 1296. The development of an effective military strategy is the most significantly innovative area of the administrators' efforts,[31] and the ability of John Comyn to extract such reasonable terms as he did in 1304 speaks volumes for the partial success of the Scots in the field, even though their policies proved inadequate to the task of defeating the English in general engagements. The continual low-intensity war conducted by the Scots after the Battle of Falkirk may have been unglamorous, but it was effective.

Fiona Watson prefaces her book *Under the Hammer* with a quotation from Edmund Burke: 'I venture to say no war can be long carried on against the will of the people.' This is surely crucial to our understanding of the Scottish capitulation of 1304 – after seven years the Community considered that the struggle had continued long enough, at least for the time being. The capitulation brought a close to hostilities between the 'official' Balliol party and the Plantagenet party, but some men, most notably of course William Wallace, were either excluded or excluded themselves from the terms of the agreement. Wallace remained active until his capture in 1305, but in the next year Bruce was able to raise forces to make an attempt on the throne. The men he enlisted may have been motivated by their support for the inheritance rights of a Scottish nobleman, but it is much more probable that the majority of the early recruits were motivated by potential gains of war and by nationalist, or at least xenophobic, sentiment, rather than by the technicalities of succession disputes. It would seem that the people, or a large enough portion of them anyway, were willing to carry on the war in 1306; whether that means that all of those people were solely, or even primarily, moved by their belief in the rights of Robert Bruce is a different question.

Were the Guardianships a successful experiment in maintaining the government of the country in a time of crisis? The answer has to be a guarded 'yes', assuming that the political independence of medieval Scotland was a laudable object. Although it is true that the Scots failed in their primary task of restoring King John and that in the final stages of their resistance the Community of the Realm were, essentially, holding out for 'reasonable' terms[32] while they still had sufficient military power to make their defeat a real challenge, they had established and maintained a Scottish government in the name of King John and had come close enough to reinstating the king to induce Robert Bruce's defection to Edward.[33] Though Robert Bruce may not have been a particularly important figure at the time, his departure to the Plantagenet cause must have had a destabilising effect on the Scottish administration. However, it did not degenerate into a Comyn interest group but retained a broad support among the different factions and family affinities among the nobility and the burgesses. There has, perhaps, been a tendency to see the Guardianships as a temporary measure, to keep the Scottish cause alive until Robert Bruce was in a position to assume the Crown. The Guardians did not labour to preserve the country for King Robert, but for King John; their contribution to the kingship of Robert I was probably a vital one, but it was not intentional.

The practical reaction of the Scottish political community to the collapse of King John's rule in the summer of 1296 was both rapid and effective, bearing in mind the challenges presented by poor communications, an occupation government, internal political divisions and the absence of an extensive body of influential and powerful men who were passing their time as prisoners of war in English castles. Its political reaction puts Scotland 'amongst the most conceptually advanced nations of medieval Europe',[34] a far cry from the popular perception of Scotland as a wild and crude backwater.

The Scots fought to preserve their customs and traditions against one of the most powerful nations in Europe for seven years. For most of that period the Guardians managed to do without either William Wallace or Robert Bruce, but it is difficult to see how the Guardianship would have become a reality without Wallace, or how the Bruce kingship could have been established without the tradition of resistance developed by the Guardians. The range of factors that led individual Scots to accept or reject Balliol or Plantagenet (and, after 1306, Bruce) lordship was immense – a maze of social, familial, cultural, economic and political pressures – but for the majority of the men in the Plantagenet camp there was no conflict of personal issues: they were in Scotland to serve their king, Edward I of England.

Edward did not move on Scotland at random, and it is important to give some thought as to why he should have chosen to do so. There has been a tendency among English historians to assume that English kings traditionally aspired to making one kingship effective throughout the British Isles. It would be difficult to make a case that English kings prior to Edward I saw British unification as either a priority or a practical proposition, or even that they were terribly interested at all, though no doubt all of them would have been happy to accept the annexation of their neighbours had the opportunity presented itself. The opportunity did not exactly present itself to Edward – he manipulated the situation to give himself opportunities to intervene in Scotland. He may have largely observed the letter of his various commitments to the Scots during the succession dispute of 1291–92, but it is easy to obey the letter of the rule when you are the person who interprets the rule. For Edward to seek to extend his influence and sovereignty was no more than his duty, as it would be for any other medieval king. If he genuinely chose to believe that English kings were the feudal superiors of Scottish ones, he must have been very selective about the evidence he chose to disregard, but for him to advance his cause, and thereby, in medieval perception, his country, was a natural obligation.

The question remains, however: what did Edward want Scotland *for*? The ideological position of increasing the bounds of a kingdom because it was a 'natural' aspect of kingship cannot have been sufficient to persuade Edward to commit large armies and vast sums of money to the acquisition of what, it would appear to us, would have been at best a domain that would only make a marginal contribution to the English Crown and at worst might become a theatre of war and a drain on the English nation for generations. The latter possibility may never have occurred to Edward. He probably expected that there would be some opposition to the deposition of King John, and some, perhaps more, to his decision to keep the government of Scotland in his own hands rather than granting it to a replacement client-king. He evidently did not think that he would face widespread revolt within a few months of his departure, or he would surely have taken measures to ensure the security of his administration. Edward's intention was to replace the Balliol kingship, not to alienate the Scottish political community. Essentially, Edward hoped to annex Scotland as a going concern, appoint a number of new managers and incorporate it into the structure of his kingship. Scotland was not to be held as a separate kingdom from England, nor was it to be held as a fief, like Edward's possessions in France. This does not answer the question of what was in it for Edward.

In 1291 Edward visited Scotland in the approach to the Great Cause. He passed through the eastern counties as far as Perth, taking fealties from landholders, ecclesiastical institutions and royal burghs. What he saw may have given him a rather misleading picture of the Scottish economy, since the towns and counties he passed through were probably the most prosperous parts of the country. The landholders and burgesses of eastern Scotland were not noticeably poorer than their counterparts in northern England. Presumably Edward, or his officials anyway, made some study of the resources of Scottish kings during his 1291 progress, and that would, no doubt, have given them a better picture of the Scottish economy; if so, the information did nothing to discourage Edward from attempting the acquisition of Scotland should the opportunity arise.

In all probability Edward believed that he could annex Scotland successfully, and he must have believed that the effort of doing so would be repaid. In the very short term, Scotland did prove to be a source of revenue – Edward was able to send a subsidy of over £4,000 to the Count of Bar from the proceeds of his 1296 campaign. Scottish kings may not have been rich but they were certainly solvent, and, since Edward's government and household already existed, the funds previously spent on several aspects of the Scottish kings' normal expenditure, such as the royal household and diplomatic matters, would now be surplus to requirements and could find their way to Edward's pocket.

Edward perhaps hoped that Scotland could be added to his domains as a personal possession, separate from England. He might be able to impose his government there permanently, without having to seek and obtain support from family and regional interest groups, but to what end?

The economy of Scotland was very much smaller than that of England, but it was, before 1296, a stable and productive entity. If Edward could annex Scotland as a sort of mammoth barony held by the Crown, he could expect an increase in revenue from rents and customs that was not subject to the interference of Parliament. The same might apply to military service. If the political community of Scotland could be induced to accept Edward's lordship, they would be liable for military service, just as they had been under Alexander III or John. Service based on land tenure did not generally extend to service abroad, but no doubt Edward would have been able to prevail on Scottish gentlemen to follow him on campaign. If he was their liege lord and was offering wages for service, there would be no reason why they should not give that service just like any other gentlemen in Edward's domains.

Since these men were already accustomed to the burden of military service and were already obliged to keep suitable arms, armour and mount, they could potentially supply a considerable body of men-at-arms to Edward's army. Research has indicated that some hundreds of landholders and burgesses in Lothian alone were liable for man-at-arms service. Lothian may have had an unusually high incidence of such duties because of the high incidence of relatively minor landholders there and because it was, by any medieval standard, a prosperous area. A great lord might, and almost invariably did, hold his estate for what was really a trivial amount of knight service; seldom more than eight or ten men, even for a great lordship or earldom. The lord or earl might, in reality, be expected to bring rather more men-at-arms to the army than their due service demanded, as a matter of personal prestige and for influence in the army, but their formal debt was not heavy.

A minor landholder with perhaps 1 per cent of the wealth of a great lord or earl and providing the service of one knight was providing the king with much more in the way of 'service per acre', so Lothian may not be a good example of a 'typical' sheriffdom. However, the amount of service available from other counties – Berwickshire, Wigtownshire, Roxburghshire, Lanarkshire and Ayrshire – does not seem to have been significantly different to that of Lothian when compared as acreages.[35]

The potential for raising substantial bodies of men-at-arms, and of course other troops as well, was quite good, but there were other military advantages to be derived from a successful conquest of Scotland. Although England and Scotland had been at peace for generations in 1295, there was no guarantee that this would always be the case. The alliance that King John made with Philip of France may have been a response to Edward's pressure – an abnormal situation – but any future Scottish king might choose to form a more aggressive alliance with the French, if they thought it might lead to the recovery of counties in the north of England that previous Scottish kings had ruled at one time and might covet in the future. The conquest of Scotland would not only provide an opportunity for recruitment, but by securing his northern border permanently Edward would be able to draw men from the north of England for service in France or Flanders in greater numbers than in the past, since he would have no fear of an invasion by the Scots.

Having made his move, Edward was committed to pursuing his objective to the utmost of his power. If he failed to bring Scotland into his domains, the damage to his prestige would be immense. Defeat by a great nation like France would be unlikely to have an immediate impact on affairs at home because an English army fighting against the French was almost inevitably going to be on campaign on the continent, not in England. Defeat at the hands of the Scots would be seen quite differently; for one thing, Scotland was hardly one of the great powers of medieval Europe, and for another, unlike France, it had a shared border with England. A successful Scottish army might not be able to impose its will on the king of England (too much of his wealth lay in areas beyond the reach of any Scottish force), but the failure of the king to protect his subjects would be detrimental to his image as a just and competent monarch. An ambitious king, and Edward was certainly that, needed to be able to attract the support of his subjects, or at least most of them, most of the time, to procure the money and manpower that his plans demanded. Edward may not have been much moved by the sufferings of his subjects in Northumberland and Cumbria, or by that of his clients and adherents in Scotland, but he could not ignore them without compromising his reputation for good lordship.

9

DEATH AND IMMORTALITY

Whatever else can be said about William Wallace, his place as a great hero, perhaps the greatest hero of the cause of Scottish independence, is secure. In part, his reputation rests on his solid and unquestioned commitment to the cause of John I and the political liberty and prestige of Scotland, in part his reputation as a 'bonnie fechter'(a fine warrior). As we might expect with a heroic figure of such stature, his reputation is further enhanced by a great deal of wishful thinking.

Historians of a socialist or Marxist sympathy can be forgiven for their tendency to see Wallace as a man of the common people; in short, a 'working class hero' – in the terms of Lennon if not of Lenin. The roots of such views are easy to identify. Wallace was not a great lord, he was prepared to confront the magnates to further his political ambitions, and he resisted the king of England. A somewhat sentimental analysis of these facets of his life has endeared Wallace to political radicals since the days of the Chartists, if not before. Even the most cursory examination of the life and acts of Wallace in the context of the society in which he lived undermines any claims for Wallace as an egalitarian liberal. The bones of the premise are certainly very real indeed – Wallace did confront the traditional influence of the magnates and he most certainly opposed, perhaps even frustrated, the expansionist policies of Edward I by upholding the cause of the Balliol kingship and thereby the cause of the political independence of Scotland. However, it is crucial to bear in mind that Wallace was both a man of his times (as all men are, at the end of the day) and a man of the aristocracy, though of a very low degree.

The 'gentle birth' of William Wallace made him a member of the governing class, not a servant of it. However humble in his degree of nobility, Wallace would probably have been quite prepared to take the head off anyone who had the temerity to suggest that he was not of noble birth. Throughout medieval Europe, such a suggestion to a man of his rank would have been 'fighting words' to say the least. More so, perhaps, because there was no great economic divide between the lower nobility and successful peasant farmers, let alone between the nobility and the burgesses. Despite a 'low' social status within the nobility, Wallace actually had more in common socially and culturally with aristocratic enemies of similar status among the Plantagenet party than with the average Scottish commoner. Almost all of the latter were field workers or low-status urban labourers; they had little common ground with the men of the privileged classes who provided administration – social, fiscal, military and judicial – throughout medieval European societies generally. The nobility, on the other hand, shared a great deal of common experience. Although the details of their rights and responsibilities varied from one individual to the next, let alone from one country to another, the extent of their duty and of their privilege varied more in degree than in nature, depending on their social, cultural, economic – and therefore political – status within the noble community.[1]

William Wallace has attracted a great deal of attention from interested enthusiasts, but surprisingly little from historians. Of the several biographies readily available at the time of writing, not one has been written by anyone with a background in medieval history generally, let alone with any scholarly understanding of the society in which Wallace lived. The lack of an understanding of the context has led to the easy acceptance of material that is at best questionable and at worst fraudulent.

This is most evident in the film *Braveheart*. Not content with relying on Blind Harry's largely fictitious poem *The Wallace* as the sole source of material, the writer, Randall Wallace, simply changed the story to suit a script that made no sort of historical sense and has, in fact, deprived Scottish people of part of their history by effectively undermining the factual material. The benefit of the *Braveheart* phenomenon is of course the extent to which it has heightened interest in medieval Scotland – an important consideration in a country where there is no viable programme of history in schools. Although *Braveheart* did help to make Scots more aware of their past, the damage done to our perception of Wallace and of the early period of the Wars of Independence is incalculable. If it is true that a picture paints a thousand words, how damaging is it when the picture is a fantasy?

Many readers will have seen pictures of armoured knights being lowered on to their chargers by means of a block and tackle and a set of sheerlegs. The pictures may have been very well executed, but the premise is nonsensical. Armies did not carry large arrays of engineering equipment simply to enable cavalrymen to get mounted. Practical demonstrations of the ability of a middle-aged man (such as this writer), little accustomed to armour and only a little more accustomed to horses, encountering no difficulty whatsoever in getting mounted draw the defence that 'armour was heavier then', which is simply untrue – the weight to volume relationship of steel has not changed appreciably in the last 700 years. The same applies to the oft-repeated observation that an armoured man who had the misfortune to fall over would have been unable to stand without the help of an assistant. No one can realistically accept that men went into battle wearing equipment so heavy that they would be completely compromised if they should happen to slip.

The *Braveheart* film takes this problem to an extreme degree. The costumes worn by the Scots were, presumably, chosen by a design team with an extensive background in Brigadoon studies – they certainly bear no resemblance whatsoever to the clothing of medieval Scots. The same applies to other visual aspects of the film. It can only be presumed that the project was carried out without any of the benefits of historical research into the clothing, housing, social and political conditions or military practices of fourteenth-century Scotland and England.

Mel Gibson was perfectly honest about the production values of the project. He described the film as being his 'fantasy' of William Wallace and his many adventures. This is a fair point – none of us would expect that a film about any romantic hero from history would necessarily have any great claims to historical validity. For one thing, a movie is not a documentary, for another, *Braveheart* was made before the current, and highly laudable, vogue for visually convincing sets and action, as exemplified by *Saving Private Ryan* or *Gettysburg*. All the same, unwittingly or otherwise, *Braveheart* has made an enormous contribution to a romantic 'kailyard' ('cabbage patch' – a Scottish term denoting literature with a romantic and rather parochial flavour) vision of medieval Scotland that historians find almost impossible to dislodge with mere evidence. Quite why it should have made so great an impression is impossible to say, though the involvement of a major Hollywood star in a heavily promoted production must surely be part of the explanation. What is harder to account for is the reaction of audiences. A medieval historian attending a screening of the film at the town of Alnwick, Northumberland, was disconcerted when the audience cheered Wallace enthusiastically as he unleashed his men to sack and destroy ... Alnwick, Northumberland!

Normally enthusiasm engendered by a history film dies out quickly, as the film recedes in public memory or as it is increasingly 'debunked' by students of the period concerned. For reasons unknown, *Braveheart* has lasted the pace more than most. In 2001 re-enactors attending an event at Bannockburn were astonished – and not a little put out – when they discovered that a man dressed as Mel Gibson (in the sort of costume he wore in the film, and complete with blue face paint) had put himself at the head of their procession. Given that most, if not all, of the re-enactors had taken a great deal of trouble to provide themselves with reasonably appropriate arms, armour, footwear and clothing, they were understandably rather less than impressed. When approached, this 'Mel Gibson' character was able to defend himself on the grounds that the makers of a film – expert professionals – were bound to be more thoroughly informed about Scottish medieval society than historians, none of whom, as he accurately pointed out, had ever 'taken *Braveheart* seriously as history'.

Inevitably there is a danger in writing history for the cinema or stage. The needs of the narrative do not always coincide with the parameters of recorded history. A similar outcome can be identified from other productions and from other artistic genres. The average person's view of the First World War is probably the product of the poems of a small number of middle-class poets, men from a privileged background with no previous military experience and a very insecure understanding of the strategic or tactical issues facing their commanders. The other 'popular' experience of the same conflict is the musical and film production *Oh What a Lovely War*. It is a fine work of art, but is of less than zero value as an insight into the 1914–18 conflict – not only does the picture fail to give a realistic view of the practical nature of the conflict on the Western Front, but it ignores the other fronts entirely and promulgates an inaccurate (and fundamentally dishonest) representation of the commanders and their staffs as being universally incompetent, uncaring, ignorant, bloodthirsty and stupid. The only way to combat that lack of reality is to read the history of the period rather than the poems. The poetry of the First World War does constitute useful, even vital material, but it is only one strand of the experience, and in no sense a common one. The same principle applies to the life and career of William Wallace. The poetry and romance of medieval Scottish writers are a part of the history and historiography of the Wars of Independence, but only a part.

Unfortunately, the search for Wallace in the history section of the local bookshop, or even library, is unlikely to yield very much of interest, unless the reader is willing to undertake a fairly extensive programme of reading. Inevitably, since it is the only source to contain any extensive material, real or fictitious, relating to his early life, scholars and enthusiasts alike have been drawn to Blind Harry. Like Mel Gibson and Randall Wallace, Harry had his own agenda; each of these men has or had a shared interest in portraying Wallace as heroic beyond the normal behaviour of men. The chief difficulty in using *The Wallace* as source material lies in the indisputable fact that it is largely fictional. Sadly, several writers have chosen to disregard that aspect of Blind Harry's work, preferring Harry's confabulations 150 years after the death of his principal character to analysis based on reliable material from record sources. This should not come as a surprise to students of medieval history generally, or to Scottish medievalists in particular.

The tradition of presenting invented romance as informed research has a long and ignoble tradition both in Scotland and, distressingly, in the rest of the world too. This can be demonstrated easily by a swift glance at the titles on the 'Scottish History' shelf in virtually any bookshop that has such a section. There are many titles in print which describe, in considerable detail, the arrival of refugee Knights Templar, who, escaping from persecution in France, escaped to Scotland with vast amounts of treasure in a fleet of seven ships.[2] In gratitude for the shelter given to them by King Robert, these renegade Templars arrived en masse at the Battle of Bannockburn to rescue the king in the nick of time, before heading off to build a mystical and mysterious chapel at Roslin and eventually turning themselves into Free Masons. These tales were first invented by one James Burnes, a nineteenth-century romanticist. There was, of course, absolutely no substance whatsoever to these stories, and they were comprehensively rebutted at the time, but they have been reheated and served up again and again by several twentieth-century writers in the guise of history.

To what extent these literary efforts are fantasies, and evidence of a complete lack of understanding (or research) of medieval history on the part of the authors, and to what extent they show a desire to make a fast and essentially fraudulent buck is difficult to say. If there is a modern mystery about William Wallace it is to be found in the fact that none of the Templar novelists has – so far – decided that Wallace was a secret Templar, though perhaps it is tempting fate to put both 'Wallace' and 'Templar' into the same sentence.

It is difficult to see quite why there have been no academic biographies of Wallace, certainly none that are really adequate for use by serious students of the period. The volume that most frequently appears on undergraduate reading lists, Andrew Fisher's *William Wallace*, is not really suitable for the purpose and many Scottish history undergraduates have had to have this explained to them, often as part of the process of telling them that their essay or exam answer was unsatisfactory. The volume in question is certainly far from being a reliable portrayal of either Wallace or the society in which he lived – it is merely the least bad of a poor selection. This is the danger of writing of an individual, a location or a period in history – any period – without endeavouring to acquire a valid understanding of the society involved.

For many writers, an important element in their evaluation of Scottish society lies in the nature of the relationship between the 'Anglo-Norman' or 'Feudalist' upper class and the downtrodden 'Scots'. These two classes, separated by language as well as status, are brought together – unwillingly in the case of the nobles – under the leadership of William Wallace, who for the purpose of popular biographies was not, presumably, a member of the 'Anglo-

Norman' ruling caste. The problems with this view are legion. First and foremost, no historian worthy of the name would think of Edward I, let alone his Scottish adversaries, as 'Anglo-Norman'. When Edward I came to the throne of England the conquest was already more than 200 years in the past. Names of French origin dominate English records of the day – they continue to do so in the twenty-first century – but the bearers of those names are not of French nationality.[3] Since the Wallace family had clearly been resident in Scotland for well over 100 years by the time William was born, we can surely accept that they were Scots, but the name Wallace is unquestionably one of 'Anglo-Norman' derivation. Should we therefore assume that Wallace was in fact a member of an Anglo-Norman elite that had displaced the native Scots aristocracy? Should we therefore also assume – because of his name and the evidently English/French ancestry of one part of his family background – that he was in fact a French-speaking aristocrat? It is difficult to see how John Balliol and Robert Bruce could have been Anglo-Normans but William Wallace a Scot, given that all three shared very similar origins.

Simple anti-factual statements, repeated at regular intervals by enthusiastic writers with little or no understanding of medieval societies, have done a great deal to promote widespread assumptions and beliefs that cannot be substantiated from what is known about medieval societies and individuals. This is the approach favoured by several populist writers who have sought to promote or denigrate particular historical figures at the expense or to the detriment of others. This approach is often used to avoid actually studying the period in question in any degree of detail, and leads to outrageously silly statements like this one:

There were those magnates, like Patrick, Earl of March and the Constable himself, who chose to support Edward out of their own volition, and there were those magnates who were, in fact, more English than Scots anyway. In this category came the elder earl of Carrick, who, despite his marriage to a Celtic heiress, Marjorie of Carrick, was probably born at Writtle near Chelmsford ...[4]

It is almost difficult to know where to start. First and foremost, neither the Earl of March nor the constable were in much of a position to offer any resistance to Edward I in the wake of the invasion of 1296. The Earls of Dunbar remained supporters of the Plantagenet party until their defeat in 1314, but since the earldom was located in the very heart of the occupied territories and was therefore surrounded by English garrisons, this can hardly be seen as choosing to support the occupation 'out of their own volition'. Who the magnates were that were 'more English than Scottish' is an excellent question, and one whose answer is unknown to medievalists. The example offered by the writer is one Robert Bruce, father of another Robert Bruce, the one that would eventually become king of Scotland. The Bruces certainly owned property in Essex, and it is quite possible that Robert senior was born at Writtle, though, as far as is known to academic Bruce biographers, there is no secure evidence to suggest that possibility. The writer's understanding of medieval society may not have been sufficiently well-developed for him to be aware that though a cat can be born in a stable, it does not become a horse. Also, Robert Bruce senior was married to Marjorie, Countess of Carrick – he was not, himself, the Earl of Carrick, merely the bearer of the title in right of his wife. The Robert who would eventually become king of Scotland in 1306 was the first Bruce to be Earl of Carrick in his own right. Curiously, few writers have seen any relevance in the fact that Robert I's mother was unquestionably a Gael – the link with his ancestors who had lived in France two centuries before would seem to be considered more significant than the fact that Robert I was the scion of a Celtic dynasty, as well as of a Lowland Scottish one with roots in eleventh-century Normandy.[5]

The belief, repeated by several writers, that the Scottish nobility spoke Norman French is easily dispensed with. There is no point in Scottish history where French can be identified as the normal language of government. Evidence for French speech among the leaders of Scottish society in the late thirteenth and early fourteenth centuries is limited to two examples of dubious value. The first is a French claim that the Scottish king spoke French. It would be very likely indeed that any well-educated gentleman (and kings would most assuredly see themselves as being of 'gentle' birth) would be able to read French, if not speak it. That does not mean that it was either their only language or their language of choice. French was the language of intellectual literature, the international language of the day. It would be ridiculous to assume that all of the English-speaking people of today were *primarily* English-speakers. English is the language of computers and films, of jazz and rock and roll; its primacy as the 'literary' language of the young all over the world can hardly be denied. There are very few educated young Netherlanders, Belgians, Swedes or Germans who do not have a reasonable grasp of the English language, but that does not compromise their nationality, though perhaps it could be construed as a result, in part, of the omnipresence of MTV and CNN. Naturally, it is quite possible that the French observer deduced that King John was a French-speaker because John spoke French to him, since it was easier than attempting to communicate in English.

The other example is derived from Barbour's epic biography of Robert I. When beset by his enemies during his sojourn in the hills after the Battle of Methven, Barbour has King Robert read aloud to his followers from a 'romance'.[6] It might be a little rash to simply assume that any romance in the early fourteenth century would most likely be written in French, but it would not be entirely unreasonable, since the vast majority of surviving medieval romances were indeed written in that language. This is a very long way from being evidence that Robert I was even a habitual French-speaker (as opposed to a reader), and we should be in no doubt at all that Robert I would have spoken middle Scots, a form of English, as his first language, as did the rest of the Scottish gentry and baronage. Their ability to communicate with their servants and tenants would have been compromised somewhat if they did not have a common language between them.

This has implications for our understanding of those lords with interests in the north and west of Scotland. Although the English language was well established throughout most of southern and eastern Scotland (and had been for centuries, if place name evidence is anything to go by), Gaelic was still the first – and only – language of a very great proportion of Scots throughout the rest of the country. Lords in the west Highlands or the Isles, however 'Norman' or 'French' their surname, would have a very complicated life indeed if they could not speak Gaelic themselves. The basic mechanics of life would require the ability to give orders, if nothing more. However, it was a common practice in both Gaelic- and English-speaking families to 'farm out' their male children to other house-holds, where they would learn the social and practical skills associated with their station in life in a less cosseted situation that they might experience at home – not hugely different in principle to the practice of packing boys off to boarding school. It would seem very unlikely indeed that a youth living in a castle in Argyllshire in the fourteenth century would fail to acquire the language of the community in which he lived. For practical reasons, therefore, it would be reasonable to assume that, far from living in a French-speaking sub-community, a modest proportion of Scottish landholders would have needed, for practical purposes, command of both English and Gaelic.

Significantly, Barbour's *Bruce*, which was unquestionably written for a noble audience, was written in Scots little more than fifty years after the events it portrays. Although it is vaguely possible that there had been a vast social change among the Scottish aristocracy in the fourteenth century that had led to the universal adoption of the Scots language in place of French, it would seem very unlikely that such a change should take place without any comment whatsoever at the time, nor that it would fail to have made any recognisable impact on the body of surviving records.

The more we examine the evidence for 'Anglo-Norman' lordship in late-medieval Scotland, the more elusive it becomes. It is certainly the case that Scottish kings of the twelfth century encouraged immigration among English landholding families and that many of the great magnate families (and many more of the minor noble families) of Scotland had antecedents of English and Anglo-Norman origin. Often these origins can be identified in the surname of the family, but evidence of that nature is both unreliable and misleading. Many of these 'migrant' family groups made their appearance in Scotland through the patronage of Scottish kings and magnates, but it should be remembered that many of these 'family groups' actually only consisted of one individual. The high incidence of those names is derived chiefly from the fact that virtually all of the incomers were men. The Scottish ladies they married did not necessarily adopt the surnames of their husbands, but their children almost invariably did. Most of these migrants entered Scottish society at a relatively exalted level; they had the resources to ensure that their children were provided for economically, generally in the form of subdivisions of the family property or acquisition of estates through marriage to heiresses, and founded their own branches of the family with distinct heritable estates, thus spreading the family name. Most importantly, these family names arrived in Scotland in the early twelfth century.

The significance of this is that the majority of the 'Anglo-Norman' families that were prominent in Scotland during Wallace's lifetime had been there for the better part of 200 years, and some of them possibly for rather longer than that, given that 'Norman' mounted soldiers served in the armies of Welsh princes some years before the Norman conquest of England. In the nineteenth century, if not before, many historians and antiquarians considered the reign of David I to be a sort of 'Norman conquest' of Scotland by the back door. Although this view has long been discredited in academic circles, the proposition still has some currency among popular writers. The purpose of the 'Norman yoke' notions among populist writers is to enhance the reputation of a heroic figure – William Wallace – by showing how constant and patriotic he was, while demonstrating the vacillating, treacherous nature of the nobility. That sort of thing has a wide appeal, but it is not an asset in the study of history, nor is it useful in a consideration of the life and career of William Wallace, who was, after all, a product of the very same 'Anglo-Norman' feudal aristocracy as John Balliol, Robert Bruce and John Comyn.

The number of men (and they were chiefly men) introduced to Scotland from England and the continent by Scottish kings and magnates to join the Scottish aristocracy was very small indeed – a matter of a few hundred spread over half a century or more – but there is a sense in which they loom much larger in Scottish history than their numbers would suggest. The chief attraction to Scots in importing men of noble status was to acquire the skills of modern warfare and the techniques of modern government. Eleventh-century Scotland may not have been the social and cultural backwater of Europe, but equally it was not in the forefront of contemporary administrative structures. The development of the governance structures of early Capetian France and the spread of those structures across northern and western Europe cannot be examined here, but it is clear that these structures had been widely adopted through southern and eastern Scotland before the death of David I in 1153.[7]

The vital component of these arrangements – the sort that we call feudal, though that was not a term used by medieval writers – was military service attached to land tenure. It is often assumed that these arrangements represented a formalisation of tenure conditions that had not previously existed; however, it is clearly the case that these landholdings were created from existing units that already had formal rental agreements of long standing. Most interestingly, many of these conversions substituted military service for what had previously been cash payments.[8]

It could be argued, though very superficially, that the new structures actually represented a backward step in social administration if one were to automatically accept that an economy based on currency is surely more sophisticated than one based on military service. There are two significant flaws to such an argument. Firstly, an economy in which military service plays a part is not the same thing as an economy based on military service – virtually, if not absolutely, every country in the world expects its citizens or subjects to give service in war if called upon to do so, and 'feudal' tenure was merely an expression of the contractual conditions. Moreover, a very large proportion of tenures with a military obligation were also subject to other obligations. Most landholders with contractual military duties attached to their lands – free tenants – were also required to provide their superior with advice, attendance at the hunt and suit of court duties, and a great many were obliged to provide a fixed quantity of that most desirable of commodities – money.

The other great flaw lies in the assumption that military service was, in itself, an unsophisticated arrangement. It actually had benefits for the landlord, the tenant and society as a whole. Because the landlord could remove a military tenant for failure to provide their due service, he could be reasonably confident that the service would be performed as required; because the tenants enjoyed heritable security of tenure, they could be confident that their descendants would have the benefit of the property in the future; and because heavy cavalry service was part of the fabric of Scottish society, the Scots were able to pursue their wars of liberation. Without military tenure there would have been very few Scottish men-at-arms in the thirteenth and fourteenth centuries, and without those men-at-arms there would have been very little prospect of success for the cause of Scottish independence, since man-at-arms service was the mainstay of the day-on-day pursuit of the war and the only viable means of countering the men-at-arms of the English garrisons. Both the literature and the records of the fourteenth century are very clear in that regard. The literature is full of the martial deeds of the political communities and the record material is full of their martial needs: wages, horse valuations and restorations, arms, ransoms, muster rolls and postings.

There were drawbacks to the system, of course. Although the level of knight service for properties was never high in relation to the value of the estate, and although the quantity of service was very seldom, if ever, changed, the cost of the service was not static. It is clear that what was expected of a man-at-arms in the way of horse and equipment quality changed considerably during the later thirteenth century.[9] The landholder might still be only liable for the service of one knight, but the cost of equipping that knight was rather greater than it had been in the past. If the landholder was to perform the service in person, he would need to spend much more than his predecessors; if he chose not to, or was unfitted to so through gender, age or infirmity, the cost of hiring a substitute would be that much more than in the past. In a simple but very effective sense, land tenure for military service was a hedge against inflation, and one that for most landholders at least was acceptable, since the rise in agricultural produce prices in the period that had elapsed since the original charter had been granted – often the better part of two centuries – more than offset the rising price of a suitable mount and arms.

Broadly speaking, land tenure by military service served Scotland well throughout the later thirteenth and the fourteenth century. The significance of great field actions like Falkirk or Bannockburn can be exaggerated all too easily; neither really changed the course of the war, after all. The normal practice of war in Scotland, particularly in the periods 1298–1304, 1312–28 and from 1333 onward, was largely similar to war in other parts of Europe – it was conducted by surprisingly small numbers of men. The chief striking arm of the forces involved was of men-at-arms, and those men-at-arms were drawn almost exclusively from the ranks of the nobility and, to a lesser extent, the burgesses. Without the active support of a large enough proportion of the noble and commercial classes, neither Balliol, Plantagenet or Bruce kings could hope to acquire and retain power in Scotland.

The military-political class was far from universally constant in their allegiance to Scottish kingship, but equally far from being constant in their allegiance to the Plantagenets. This phenomenon was not limited to the Scottish nobility. Subjects of the kings of England in their capacity as French lords became increasingly fluid in their allegiance throughout the fourteenth and fifteenth centuries. More significantly, in the second and third decades of the fourteenth century, several English lords in the north of England became sufficiently disenchanted with their own kings to choose to seek the lordship of Robert I, approaching him for confirmation of their charters and the like, perhaps for fear that Northumberland, Cumbria and Westmorland might be annexed by the Scots.[10] It would be rash to conclude that such incidents were evidence that certain areas of northern England were diffident about their nationality, or that a Scottish administration in Northumberland and Cumbria would have been considered acceptable to the political communities of those counties, but it would be reasonable to assume that the landholders of northern England might be prepared to accept the imposition of Robert I's rule if he could offer them the stability and protection that Edward II was very evidently failing to provide. We should not think for a moment that Northumberland men seeking the protection of Robert I were in any sense unpatriotic; they were responding to circumstances over which they had no real influence, let alone control.

The issue of the constancy – or otherwise – of the Scottish nobility is one of great importance in any evaluation of the life and career of William Wallace. Both the Balliol and Plantagenet parties were aware that the support of the noble and commercial classes was crucial to their prospects. These were the classes that provided the backbone of civil and military administration. Naturally, both parties strove to enlist the local political community in their respective causes and therefore offered incentives, coercion, persuasion or a mixture of the three to achieve this. Landholders could of course flee to another area if they felt they could not accord with the current source of authority, but they could hardly take their lands with them; if they wanted to stay on their estates – a natural desire at any time, but of huge social and cultural significance 700 years ago – they simply had to accept the government of the day or face forfeiture.

The incentives to support whichever party was currently in the ascendant in a particular vicinity were possibly as significant as the disincentives. Alignment with the 'current dispensation' obviously secured title to land, but there were also opportunities within the administration. Jury service and some military service were obligations on most landholders, but the demand for men-at-arms invariably outstripped the supply, so there were generally employment and career opportunities with the army – particularly the English army, since wages seem to have been a rarity in Scottish ones. Local stability was vital to the local economy, and landholders might well be prepared to ignore their personal political inclinations for the sake of the continuing commercial viability of their property, as well as the wellbeing of their relatives and tenants. These were crucial elements in the process of deciding political alignment at a given moment. As the incumbent of the chief property of a family network, the lord or lady of the property would have to take some cognisance of the effect that their own political allegiance might have on the other members of the family.

All in all, administrations of all parties seem to have been content to distinguish between different branches of the same family; just because some members of the Ramsay or Douglas families or their allies were in the peace of the Plantagenets did not prevent other members of those families from being in the peace of Robert I or David II, but while an individual might declare for one cause because the bulk of their lands were in areas under the administration of that party, other lands in their possession in areas in the control of the other party would obviously be at risk. If those lands were in the hands of tenants, rather than kept 'in hand' by the landholder, the opposing government might choose to leave the tenant in place so long as they continued to support the party governing that area in order to avoid having to install an alternative landholder. However, it would have been rash to rely on that being the outcome of the defection of one's superior. Any landholder with properties scattered throughout the country (and that would include a hefty proportion of all the magnates) would have to give very careful consideration to the fortunes of others before making a change of allegiance, since their own defection might well lead to the forfeiture of family members and friends – the very people who, in concert, provided greater lords with the military strength that validated their political prominence.

The commercially successful men and women in the urban communities were even more vulnerable to changes of administration than their rural counterparts. Landholders whose properties were declared forfeit for opposing the current administration could expect to have their estates restored as and when their own party achieved its goal, or, failing that, they could hope to reach an accommodation with the successful party. If their estates were laid waste they could hope to borrow money to restock and rebuild on the security of their land; they might be heavily in debt for some time, but the land itself was a secure asset. Families whose status was derived from commercial activity could be utterly destroyed in a matter of hours, even minutes, simply by setting fire to their premises. The family might still retain the land, but restoring a business is dependent on investment and access to the market. A family whose business had already been burnt out once would probably encounter some difficulty in raising the capital for restoration, even if they could be sure of access to the marketplace. If the occupation government had chosen to destroy someone's livelihood as punishment for political activity they were hardly likely to allow that person to retain such market privileges as they had enjoyed in the past, or even to allow them continued access to the market at all.

Curiously, although the burgesses of Scotland were just as prone to transfers of allegiance as the nobility (and everyone else for that matter), they have not suffered the same fate at the hands of historians. No author has written about the treacherous, pro-English tendencies of the burgess class, and, though a very large proportion of that class bore French or English surnames, no author has written about the 'Anglo-Norman' burgesses of Scotland, but a great many have written about the 'Anglo-Norman' nobility. By the close of the thirteenth century any division between the lesser nobility and the more successful families among the burgesses had, in any case, become rather blurred.

Noble families married their children into burghal families for the sake of good cash dowries and access to the privileges of burgess participation in commerce, and burghal families married their children into the noble landholding class in search of prestige and influence in the political, cultural and economic life of the vicinity. The pressure on the nobility to provide their children with an adequate standard of living was considerable, but so was the pressure to maintain the integrity of the family estate: an integrity that would be very rapidly compromised by permanent division of the property. A few generations of division and subdivision of the property would result in impoverishment for all, whereas the existence of a family estate empowered the current landholder both economically and politically, giving that individual a capacity to protect and further the interests of the family as a whole.

The status of a family was a vital component in the future not merely of the immediate family members of the current incumbent, but of their cousins, uncles, aunts and so on. This is an important consideration when exploring the relationship between Wallace and the clergy. A number of writers have drawn attention to the support that William Wallace enjoyed from the ecclesiastical community, in contrast to the opposition he faced from the nobility.

The distinction between the two is a false one – although it is true that men of very humble origins could make a career in the Church, their numbers were few indeed. Almost all of the beneficed clergy of Scotland, like their counterparts in England or France, were drawn from the ranks of the nobility. There were a number of reasons why this should have been the case. Admission to a monastery or to a parish was largely dependent on the ability of the candidate to find either a sum of money paid to the monastery, or to the landholder or institution which had the right of appointment (advowson) to that parish, a right often retained by landholders granting land to the Church, since it was a source, however irregular, of hard cash. It was possible for candidates to borrow money against the future income they would derive from the parish, but the majority of candidates probably gained their positions through a mixture of family connections and a money payment, which itself was likely to be borrowed from a family member.

The 'networking' aspect of family connections can be seen in Blind Harry's account of Wallace's adventures before his rise to fame. According to Bower and Blind Harry, Wallace was sheltered by two priests, each of them an uncle. It might seem unlikely that a man should have two uncles in holy orders, but there are a number of qualifying factors to be considered. For one thing, there were very many more priests in relation to the population as a whole in the late Middle Ages than there are today. In addition to perhaps 1,500 parish priests, there was an extensive hierarchy of abbots, archdeacons and bishops who, in turn, like other senior members of the noble classes, had chaplains of their own. Additionally, there was the regular clergy of the monasteries, convents and abbeys. Given the relatively limited range of career paths considered suitable for noblemen, it would not be particularly peculiar that two men in one generation of a family should become priests. Further, the terms of relationship used in medieval documents do not completely coincide with current usage. The two 'uncles' concerned need not have been the brothers of his father or mother for him to regard them as such.

The support of the two Wallace priests – and various others – has been seen as an example of a distinction that did not exist in the medieval period – namely, a social and cultural divide separating the noble and clerical establishment. In the view of one writer, the support Wallace derived from the clerical community was based on the fact that:

> Unlike the magnates, most of whom were committed to Edward's cause on account of their extensive English estates, the prelates, by and large, were men of a more independent mind. They were more likely to have risen from the ranks of the Scottish community and were therefore not so susceptible to Anglo-Norman influence.

This statement neatly encapsulates an important aspect of the general perception of Wallace, the nobles and the clergy, and is worth examining critically. The first point to make is that, as we have seen, Scottish clerics were recruited, in the main anyway, from the noble families, and the concept of 'Anglo-Norman' *anything* really has no place in either England or Scotland in the later Middle Ages. Realistically, no Scottish magnates had what we might reasonably call 'extensive' estates in England, or at least certainly not estates sufficient to make the holder a particularly important figure in the local political communities in which their properties lay, let alone give them any stature in the national political community of England. The Bruce family certainly owned estates in Essex, but their wealth, power and influence came from their Scottish properties – they may even have held a barony in that county, but so did several other people. There were undoubtedly people with properties in both countries who endeavoured to protect their inheritances by allegiance to the Plantagenet cause, but they had interests and considerations beyond immediate property rights. It was by no means clear to the Scottish political community that Edward was unquestionably acting outside his rights in 1296. King John had, after all, accepted Scottish kingship on the basis of Edward's suzerainty. Who was to say Edward did not have a right to forfeit his vassal if he failed to give the service due to his acknowledged lord?

It is true that many Scots lords served Edward against the Balliol cause and later against the Bruce cause, but it is more difficult to demonstrate their willingness to serve the Plantagenet cause when they had a real choice in the matter. It is very tempting for Scottish writers to take a judgemental attitude on this issue, but difficult, apparently, for them to understand that taking a patriotic stance in the face of an occupying army might have serious consequences such as loss of land, livelihood or head, not to mention the loss of any opportunity to protect the interests of the estate, the family, the tenants and the other dependants. Furthermore, lordship was a two-way relationship. The estate holders did not live in isolation from their tenants, and, in the same way that the great lords owed a duty of counsel to the king, minor nobles had an obligation to their superiors. A strong-willed lord with good leadership skills might be able to persuade or cajole his tenants into supporting the political position that he had adopted himself, but any lord would have to give serious thought to his continued allegiance to a cause that his tenants opposed.

Lordship was hardly a democratic condition, but it was certainly rather more consensual than is generally realised. Most significantly, if the Scottish nobility were committed to the Plantagenet cause, it was a commitment that went largely unnoticed by English writers, who were clearly of the opinion that, regardless of the overt allegiance of Scottish lords, their hearts and minds were generally 'with their own people'. This is significant in two ways: firstly, because it is shows that there was a perception among the English that the support of Scottish lords for English kings was only skin-deep at the best of times, and that the bonds of lordship and tenant or dependant were of greater significance than oaths given to a foreign king who had been successful in war; but also because it clearly shows the medieval understanding of national identity – that people born and raised in a particular country were likely to have a political inclination that included the defence of that country against foreign interests. English writers, then, were clear that the shared nationality of the Scots was a major factor, perhaps even the most significant factor, in persuading the community to carry on the fight.

Even the most cursory examination of the records of English garrisons and armies in Scotland shows that many Scots did choose to support the Plantagenet party against John I – most famously, of course, Robert Bruce, Earl of Carrick, whose pattern of defection and reconciliation is positively bewildering. Unsurprisingly, the greatest concentration of consistent Plantagenet support lay in the southern regions of the country. Traditionally, this has been ascribed to the cultural and linguistic affinities of the nobility living between the Humber and the Forth, or even the Tay. There were important cultural similarities between the societies of northern England and southern Scotland, but these similarities extended throughout the communities concerned, they were not limited to the aristocracy. A farm worker in Lanarkshire did not lead a markedly different life to a farm worker in Northumberland.

The single most important factor in the establishment and maintenance of an English administration in Lothian or Roxburghshire or Dumfriesshire lay in the effectiveness of the military occupation. If the sheriff's orders could be enforced in a particular area, he could oblige the local political community to perform their due military service on pain of forfeiture. This obviously eased the manpower requirement of the administration, but it also helped to keep the local political community out of the ranks of the Balliol (or later Bruce) party. Maintaining the credibility of the occupation was undoubtedly less of a challenge in Lothian, where there was a well-developed network of strongholds and less broken country from which insurgents could operate. Also, a relatively high proportion of the population lived in towns and larger villages – Edinburgh, Haddington, Linlithgow, Winchburgh – and were therefore more vulnerable to the occupation than their compatriots in Wester Ross or Invernesshire, where English government was only achieved very briefly, if at all, and at rare intervals.

It has been suggested that the senior aristocracy of Scotland, the magnates, were more inclined toward the Plantagenet party than the population as a whole. The magnates wanted to retain their positions in Scotland and their estates in England, and were also bound by the common ideals of chivalry to the ruling class in England in a way that separated them from their fellow Scots. Naturally enough, men and women of property and influence certainly *did* want to preserve their prominence in the one and their property in the other. Neither of these issues was necessarily an issue of political allegiance in quite the simplistic way we might imagine. It was perfectly normal for wealthy men and women to invest in properties in other countries, just as they do today. English people owned property in France and vice versa. The two countries were frequently at war, which might interrupt the commercial aspects of owner-ship (though it might just as easily not) but did not, of itself, bring about the permanent loss of the property.

If the magnates were less than constant in their support of Scottish kingship at all, let alone the kingship of John I or Robert I, the same applied to the rest of Scottish society. The evidence for noble co-operation with the occupation can be seen in the act of homage or in military service in garrisons throughout Scotland, or at least those parts where garrisons were established. We should not assume that the absence of a garrison indicates an inability on the part of the occupation power to place one or maintain one – the administration may have considered that a garrison in a specified location would be unjustifiably expensive or that they had a degree of support in the local community that made a garrison unnecessary, thus saving on man-power which could be better used somewhere else.

Obviously, the influence of Scottish magnates in the Plantagenet camp was of great importance. The Earls of Dunbar were vital props to the English occupation in the south-east between 1296 and 1314, and again in 1333–34. The allegiance of the Earls of Dunbar would seem to sup-port the contention that the senior nobility were part of what E.M. Barron saw as an anglophile, southern aristoc-racy willing to compromise Scottish independence, which was duly saved by the consistent loyalty of the Gaelic/Celtic/Highland community. One might ask where that would leave the MacDougalls, who were unquestionably Gaelic, Celtic and Highland, and were also, equally unquestionably, consistent supporters of the Plantagenet occupation against Robert I after 1306.

Collaboration is an ugly and inappropriate word for the generality of the relationship between the Scots and the Plantagenet occupations of 1296–1314 and the 1330s and 1340s, but there was, without question, a great deal of practical co-operation, particularly in those areas where the occupation was well supported by castles and secure towns – inevitably, the areas where a larger proportion of the populace depended on commerce and services rather than agriculture for their livelihood. To see such co-operation as collaboration would be akin to charging every police officer, juror, lawyer, judge, local government officer and tax collector who served in France between 1940 and 1944 with being a Nazi sympathiser – there would be a grain of absurd truth to it, but it would be a gross and offensive distortion. The same applies to late-medieval Scotland during the occupations. Without some degree of co-operation with the government there would inevitably be some decay in law and order, with consequences for the commercial environment.

Furthermore, the issue applies to the whole of the community, not just the noble and the financially successful. We have already seen that a group of Scots of very low status could become aware that the Edwardian occupation might provide an opportunity to improve their lot. Petitioning Edward for the same rights as his husbandmen in England was an astute move. In the wake of victory Edward might well feel inclined to be generous, particularly in regard to a matter which, though important to the petitioners, was of no moment to himself, but it also gave Edward an opportunity to demonstrate quality of lordship in what was, in his view anyway, a fief recently recovered by its liege lord. He could be seen to be taking a real interest in the affairs of his new subjects, a good move in virtually any political arena, and a demonstration of the 'good lordship' that medieval communities needed if they were to prosper.

Acceptance of Plantagenet lordship in Scotland was not, then, a matter of class or status, or of linguistic or geographical background, though all of these were probably factors for some or even most people at one time or another. Adherence to one party or another, or even to none at all if one could get away with it, was the product of a much wider and more subtle mix of issues than we might expect. Political issues of any kind can only tell us so much about human motivation. Mankind is not especially noted for consistently rational behaviour at the best of times, and it is very likely that many active participants on either side would have struggled to explain quite why they were serving Balliol rather than Plantagenet interests, save for those whose property lay within an area that was currently secure for this party or that and who were not prepared to abandon their heritage for the sake of maintaining their allegiance to one man, regardless of whether that man represented Scottish sovereignty or English suzerainty.

Wallace's relationship with the aristocracy, or at least with those elements of the aristocracy senior in status to himself (most of them), has generally been seen as a difficult one. Fordoun, Wyntoun, Bower and of course Blind Harry made their readers aware that Wallace was not intimidated by the nobility, and that he was quite prepared to enforce their obedience by the same means as he was prepared to enforce military service from the wider population – the gallows. While this is surely the case, there are a number of issues to be considered. Wallace can be perceived as a leader who rose to prominence, despite the ill will and resistance of his social superiors, as a result of his successes in the field. Through the late spring and summer of 1297 William Wallace was able to assemble a force and conduct operations against the English; it would not be safe to assume that he was alone in doing so, merely that he was the most successful among them, though even that judgement is subject to the possibility that Wallace survived long enough to come to prominence, whereas other men who might have afforded him some competition had already fallen in the struggle.

Wallace was not the sole instigator of resistance, but a man in the forefront of the military aspect of the struggle in central Scotland. Before he and Murray effected the union of their armies at Stirling Bridge, Edward's administration in Scotland had already made him aware that all was not well there, that only one county of Scotland (Berwick) had a complete administration, 'and that only recently', and that the Scots had already appointed sheriffs and bailies in most of the others. Although Wallace was a very active man, he self-evidently could not have procured that situation by his efforts alone.

Wallace had obviously made a reputation for himself before Stirling Bridge; he had, after all, gathered an army, but he was not of great political significance. Victory over Cressingham enhanced Wallace's prestige enormously, and it is after that battle that we see more evidence of Wallace the political animal and administrator in his role as Guardian. The title would, however, have been of little value unless Wallace could depend on the political support of the existing structures of power and influence that had made the reinstatement of a Scottish administration possible. It is difficult to see how that reinstatement, even if it was very scattered, could have occurred without the complicity of a proportion of the senior aristocracy large enough to impose their will or, at the very least, strong enough to discourage immediate local opposition among the rest of the Scots.

It could be argued, and has been suggested or even asserted by some writers, that Wallace enjoyed a good relationship with the ecclesiastical authorities and that that gave him credibility among the great and good. It would seem that this was the case. However, it is most unlikely that the clerical magnates, the bishops, abbots and priors, would have had the level of influence throughout Scotland that would have been necessary to restore government in the name of King John without at least the complicity, if not the active support, of the noble community. Wallace's relationship with the Church before the Battle of Stirling Bridge was probably rather less significant than it was afterward. As Guardian, Wallace was a man worth cultivating to ensure that the rights and privileges of the Scottish clerical establishment, not to mention their treasured independence from archbishops, were preserved from English domination.

As a leader of a raiding party in early 1296 he may well have attracted the interest of senior Scottish churchmen like Bishop Wishart, but his influence over any aspect of Church matters, beyond the level of driving the odd English priest from his benefice, was probably very slender. It is, in any case, important to remember that the political 'estate' of the clergy may have been nominally separate from that of the nobility, but almost all of the priests, monks and nuns who composed the Scottish clergy were members of noble families. To a very great extent, the priorities, beliefs and cultural and social practices of one were also the practices of the other. It would be very unlikely indeed that the clergy as a class would adopt a radically different posture from the nobility. Wallace was, however, aware of the value of ecclesiastical support, both moral and financial. His intervention to secure the election of William Lamberton as bishop of St Andrews was not simply a matter of denying the preferred candidate of Edward I, but of encouraging the patriotic party within the Scottish Church.

The popularity of Wallace in the wider community, and in the army in particular, must be seen as an important, even crucial, element in his rise to the Guardianship, but he could not be everywhere at once. To make his rule a reality, he would have needed the co-operation of the administrative, judicial and military practitioners of the community – the nobles and burgesses. To an extent, this can be encompassed in traditional Wallace hagiography – the magnates reject Wallace but the minor gentry, most of whom would seem to have been either Wallace's cousins or his uncles, if Blind Harry is to be taken at face value, took him to their hearts. The flaw in that rationale is, of course, that the minor and major lords did not exist in either social, cultural, political or financial isolation from one another. In certain regions, most noticeably Lothian, there were no great lords, but a great many minor ones who held their property directly from the Crown, not through an intermediary.[11]

In the north and west, where lordships and earldoms tended to be much larger, there was much more subinfeudation, and thus a greater degree of dependence of lesser lords on greater ones. It would be a courageous, not to say foolhardy, action for a minor lord to give his support to

Wallace and the Balliol cause without the approval of his superior. As we have seen already, English chroniclers were inclined to think that Scottish magnates were not loyal to King Edward, even when they were present in his army or otherwise active in his cause. They may well have been right to do so: when the Earl of Strathearn made captives of the MacDuff men who had been intent on capturing him, he did not pass them over to the occupation government. Had the earl been confident of Edward's victory and Wallace's defeat, he would not have dared to withhold them from the Plantagenet administration.

If the earl's decision is not an indication of Scottish perception of the security of the Plantagenet government, the action of the MacDuff men in attacking the earl certainly is. Evidently the occupation was not strong enough to overawe opposition, and therefore not able to offer the 'good lordship', the political and economic stability, on which long-term retention of political power depended. The MacDuff/Strathearn incident also shows that opposition to Edward's government was not limited to the actions of Sir William Wallace, nor to the labouring classes and the minor nobility, nor to the activities of 'Celtic' Scotland. It may have been sporadic, but it was widespread, both socially and geographically.

If we accept that Wallace was only one of a number of captains of followings in the spring and early summer of 1297, it is crucial to give some consideration to how he became the leader of a national movement rather than a minor leader within it. Success is an excellent recruiting officer, and it would seem that William Wallace was effective in battle. That would be enough to draw men to him, but whether they would be the men he required was a different matter. All of Wallace's early engagements seem to have been carried out by men-at-arms. They may not all have enjoyed the social status that would normally be associated with man-at-arms service, but they were described by a senior officer of the occupation government as being 'well armed' and 'well mounted' – in the medieval sense of 'armoured', and mounted on beasts suitable for the purpose.

No doubt many of the men who sought service (or just adventure) with Wallace were unable to acquire the equipment or the skills to serve as men-at-arms, but self-evidently there were enough of them to provide Wallace with a force able to conduct successful mobile operations on a more or less continuous basis. Such a force need not have been very large to pose a real and continuing threat to the occupation. Most garrisons were very small indeed, and even a band of just thirty or forty men-at-arms would be enough to put them on the defensive. Even if the garrison ran to as many as forty men-at-arms, and few of them did, it would hardly be prudent to commit the entire cavalry element of the garrison to the pursuit of an enemy that might be strong enough to offer battle and win it – a possibility that would be very detrimental to the credibility of the administration, both locally and nationally. Locally it would undermine the power of the sheriff and nationally it would provide good propaganda material for the Balliol cause.

The mobile force that Wallace raised and led in early 1297 probably included men whose status would not normally have led them to man-at-arms service, but who had through whatever means – service in foreign armies, experience of brigandage – become soldiers. Such men were likely few and far between. Also, few men would have been willing to commit themselves to absolutely continuous service, so it is reasonable to assume that the majority of the early force was drawn from the noble classes – men with the experience, training, social background and economic muscle to serve as men-at-arms. Given how small the force is likely to have been, a matter of dozens or scores rather than hundreds and thousands, it is quite possible that a fair proportion of them were members of the wider Wallace family, but even if the force was as small as thirty it would be very unlikely that the Wallace family would have been able to fill its ranks. Nor is it likely that all of them would have been 'in capite' tenants – that is to say, men who held their land directly from the king. Some of them, at least, would have been the tenants and dependants of other men; some of them of magnates. Service with Wallace would be very hard to explain to a superior whose allegiance – currently and officially anyway – lay with Edward I.

Situations where inferiors and superiors differed in their political allegiance were naturally fraught with difficulties for both parties. The forfeiture of a tenant who had turned out for the opposition might undermine the prestige of the superior with his other tenants. If the tenant happened to be a family member that would obviously complicate the issue further – how difficult would it be to forfeit own your son or daughter? Forfeiture of a particularly popular landholder might not go down too well with the farm tenants or among the local political community. Additionally, the replacement of forfeited tenants with men whose political inclinations seemed to be more reliable might be very counterproductive in the long term, should it become necessary for the superior to defect or accept a change in the administration due to developments either at a local level, such as the fall of a particular stronghold, or at a national level, in the event of a truce being made at an inconvenient juncture for the landholder. Failure to forfeit recalcitrant tenants would not play well with the administration, of course, but then the security of the administration, whether Plantagenet or Balliol, might not be all that secure. It might fall to the opposition, in which case having one or more tenants already in the allegiance of the new administration might provide a means of negotiating an accommodation that would preserve their position in the community and, of course, their tenure. Another important aspect of forfeiture, or rather of granting property, was that the new tenant would have to establish their authority. In peacetime this was probably easy enough to achieve, but forfeitures were very rare in peacetime; in a period of prolonged if intermittent warfare, imposing lordship may well have been a rather more challenging proposition.

The business of protecting and furthering the interests of a family group was, then, a complex and difficult process. The lords who accepted Edward I's kingship in 1296 had very little choice if they were to retain their heritages in the short term. If Edward were to achieve his goal, their properties would be secure in the long term as well, but Edward might not be able to make his rule a reality. In the summer of 1297 it was fast becoming evident that Edward was not going to achieve an easy assimilation of Scotland, and might even be defeated and his administration driven out. In the event of a Scottish victory, even a temporary one, landholders, even prominent magnates, might find themselves forfeited by the Balliol kingship if they had become too closely associated with the occupation and were seen as being too hostile to the Balliol cause for a realistic reconciliation. If they were unfortunate enough to be captured, they might even get hanged for treason – Wallace did.

The Battle of Stirling Bridge gave Wallace a degree of political acceptability, not to mention popular acclaim.

It did not turn him into a magnate, but it gave him enough status to be credible as a leader for the Balliol cause. Military success gave him political office, but it was not anticipated initially that Wallace would act as the sole Guardian; he was to share the burden with his companion in arms Sir Andrew Murray. Murray's death some weeks later left Wallace to get on with it himself, very probably a situation of his own choosing. Had he wanted to share the Guardianship, there would have probably been plenty of willing candidates. It would, perhaps, have been a challenge to find someone who was acceptable to all of the different elements of the Balliol party, but there seems to have been no action on Wallace's part to involve anyone else in wielding executive power.

Clearly, his defeat at Falkirk undermined Wallace's political stature fatally. Even if he had retained the support of the magnates and the clerical establishment, and despite the fact that he still enjoyed a good deal of popularity in what remained of the army, Wallace was definitely yesterday's man, politically and militarily. He had endeavoured to fight a war of manoeuvre and major engagements and had been defeated. The army he had raised had been thoroughly beaten, to such a degree that the Scots would have to adopt a different approach to the war.

The 'revolutionary' and 'guerrilla' tactics attributed to Wallace by historians were in fact totally conventional practice for the thirteenth and fourteenth centuries. Instead of the great forces that had met at Falkirk or Stirling, both the Scots and the English came to rely on the services of men-at-arms. The return to conventional warfare also led to a return to more traditional leadership arrangements. Wallace might have been acceptable as the commander of a large force of all arms invading northern England or confronting Edward I, but in the more closely knit forces that conducted the campaigns of 1298–1304, social station may have been more significant than in the army of 1296. Senior lords with their own followings might not have the same confidence in Wallace that they would have had in a man of greater status and, perhaps, wider experience.

Defeat at Falkirk destroyed Wallace's career in executive politics and destroyed his army, but it did not change the course of the war to any great degree. Edward does not seem to have had any clear view of how best to exploit his victory. His army had been badly damaged in the battle, and there was sickness in the camps, little money to pay the troops and little for them to do if they were kept on station. Edward disbanded his army and returned to England, leaving his administration in Scotland little better off than it had been before the campaign. Wallace had been defeated and driven out of the Guardianship, but little had been recovered in the way of territory, and much of that had been lost to the Scots again almost immediately. One of the few tangible benefits had been a brief campaign in Lothian,[12] where a column under Antony Bek, Bishop of Durham, had succeeded in recapturing three castles, probably including the massive fortress of Dirleton and Yester, which had fallen to the Scots in the preceding months, possibly as far back as Wallace's passage through Lothian in November of the previous year.

Edward's victory undermined Wallace and the Balliol cause, but his own withdrawal from Scotland so quickly afterwards can have done nothing for the prestige of his kingship among the Scots. If Edward's lordship was limited to sporadic invasions of Scotland, rather than imposing firm government and stability, there was not a lot to be said for it. It probably did not do a great deal for the morale of the garrisons either. A major expedition, even if did not come to battle with the Balliol forces, would make some impression on the population in the areas that the army passed through, though not perhaps an impression likely to win hearts and minds in the community, but the return of the army to England would inevitably give an impression of weakness as well.

The Balliol party suffered a severe blow at Falkirk, but not one that destroyed either their will or their capacity to continue with the war. It could be argued that the destruction of Wallace as a political force was in fact the most significant outcome from the perspective of both parties. This rather depends on the degree of security Wallace enjoyed in the Guardianship. Wallace governed with what later Scottish writers would call 'raddure' – not perhaps oppressively, or at least not any more so than the times demanded, but with both vigour and rigour. It would be surprising if he had not managed to offend some of the men around him. His meteoric rise to power may have been sanctioned by an extensive body of opinion among the magnates, but they had not expected that Wallace would reign alone, nor would he have done but for the death of Sir Andrew Murray. The most powerful grouping in the Balliol party was based on the Comyn family, and Andrew Murray was a cousin of sorts to John Comyn, Earl of Buchan.

It would be unsafe to see Murray as a stalking horse for the Comyns, a means of keeping control over, or at least influence in, the Balliol cause. The tradition of service to Crown and country was very strong in the Comyn family; they had, after all, prospered in the service of Scottish kings and would certainly hope and expect to do so again in the event of a Balliol restoration. The leaders of the Comyn family, John, Lord of Badenoch and John, Earl of Buchan were still prisoners of war when Murray's forces seized the north, but it would be unlikely that he could have mustered the necessary support without the knowledge and assent, not to say connivance, of the network of barons, free tenants and officials with Comyn family ties that dominated the political community of north-east Scotland. The Comyns, and other northern lords as well, could reasonably expect that a man of Murray's station in life would not encourage uncontrollable mob rule and that if anything he might be able to impose better order than the English administration.

Without the acquiescence, if not support, of the Comyn interest in northern Scotland, Murray's rising might not have got very much further than the attacks on Castle Urquhart and Inverness and, however successful such attacks might be, there would be little chance of exploiting the victory to set up a national administration without a good deal of input from the nobility in general, and, at least in the north-east, the Comyn family in particular. The existence of a Scottish administration in the north, however *ad hoc* and rudimentary, was of huge significance for Balliol activists and sympathisers elsewhere. The reduction of English garrisons proved that the occupation government was not invincible, and the increasingly extensive area under Scottish administration was an indication that the war generally was not going in favour of the English – an encouraging sign for the Scots.

Wallace was able to assemble a force of some stature by August 1297, but he would have been very hard pressed to achieve a victory at Stirling Bridge without the army of the north under Murray. He probably would have been obliged to retire in front of what would have been a very much greater force than his own, abandoning the whole of the south of Scotland to the occupation.

The popular view of the Comyns is that expressed by the Scottish writers of the fourteenth century, Barbour and Fordoun. In the tale of how Robert Bruce saved the nation from the English and from treacherous Scotsmen, the Comyn family stand fair and square with the villains.[13] As relatives, neighbours and associates of the Balliol family from long before the time of the great competition for the Scottish throne, and as remarkably staunch servants of the Balliol cause through seven years of war after 1297, it is hardly surprising that they should have opposed the ambitions of the Bruce family, but they were hardly unpatriotic. Their modern reputation shows the power of propaganda, even 700 years after the event. Fordoun and Bower were both enthusiastic supporters of the Bruce cause, but Barbour was an uncritical fan. He equated the Bruce cause with the Scottish patriotic cause, thus making the political opponents of the Bruces into traitors.

The failure – as presented by contemporaries – of the Comyn men-at-arms to engage at Falkirk may have been the downfall of Wallace. Certainly his defeat undermined his political credibility but, at the same time, it is not at all likely that the Comyns left the field in the hopes of bringing about his defeat. These were not stupid men; they must have been aware that their departure would sit very badly with the community. It is infinitely more likely that they deserted from a battle that they could see was already lost. If the Comyns can be legitimately criticised for not being killed in action at Falkirk, the same criticism can be levelled at William Wallace. In reality both Wallace and the Comyns had a duty to survive the battle, in that they were the recognised representatives of the Scottish political community and the representatives of King John. Their feudal responsibilities obliged them to do their best to keep his cause alive in Scotland, not to achieve chivalric but point-less martyrdom on the battlefield.

The William Wallace encountered in historical record is far removed from the Wallace of films or enthusiastic biog-raphers. It may be evident to historians that Wallace was a man of noble lineage, a member of the ruling class (though in a relatively humble degree), but that does rather con-flict with the well-established, though erroneous, view of Wallace as a simple commoner drawn into political life by his patriotic fervour. While it is true that the magnate class did dominate political activity and leadership in Scotland – as was the case throughout northern and western Europe – men like Wallace were an integral part of the political community. The distance between the highest and lowest members of that community was one of social and eco-nomic degree, but not of class, culture or language. These aspects of his background are not evidence that Wallace was in any sense either more or less 'Scottish' than his neighbours, but seem to present a problem to those writers whose enthusiasm for Wallace the hero clouds their view of Wallace the man.

His achievements were very real. Edward I did not make Wallace the target of his ire at random; he did so because Wallace was a threat to his ambition of adding Scotland to his domains. Neither Wallace nor his successors as Guardians actually managed to either restore King John or to completely expel the English, though Blind Harry has his hero accomplish this feat, not once, but three times. They were, however, successful in preventing Edward from annexing Scotland between 1296 and 1304 and, in so doing, made Scots accustomed to the acceptance of admin-istration through Guardians rather than kings, a situation that would arise on the death of King Robert, the captivity of David II and the captivity of James I, then again during the minorities of James II, James III, James V, Mary I and James VI. The various Guardians and regents managed to maintain Scottish independence in the face of a powerful neighbour that may have learned by the middle of the fourteenth century that the physical conquest of Scotland was just too big a project for English arms, but which still had an interest, perceived or real, in keeping the Scots weak.

By the time Robert Bruce assumed the kingship, his subjects had already been at war, intermittently, for a decade. For most of that period, the existence of a Scottish political entity was made possible by the efforts of the Guardians of Scotland and by their ability to command military service from the noble and burghal communities. The first Guardianship after the deposition of King John may have collapsed little more than a year after its inauguration, but that year was critical to the fortunes of the Scots. It showed that even without the presence of a king to lead them and to fight for, a strong body of opinion in Scottish society was prepared to take up arms in defence of the political independence of the country, and that that body of opinion extended far beyond the bounds of the customary political class: the landholders, lords and clergy.

Even before he became Guardian, Wallace had proved capable of demanding and receiving military service, but after the initial stages of his military career, at the point when his force ceased to be a raiding party of armoured cavalry men (or brigands depending on one's perspective) and started to become a more conventional army, he must have depended on his personal prestige, acquired through successful actions against the occupation, as a recruiting sergeant. Many of the men who joined the army of William Wallace in the early summer of 1297 must have done so of their own volition, as a political act rather than as a path for personal ambition or through the threat of the gallows that Wallace apparently had erected in every town and village.

Although he was, by birth and upbringing, a member of that class, Wallace himself was living proof that desperate times could lead to great opportunity. His station within the noble community was low, not to say obscure, and for such a man to gain the respect of a sufficiently large portion of society that he could be entrusted with wielding the power of the Crown was remarkable, particularly since the Crown was hardly in a position to confer that authority at all, given that King John was a prisoner in England.

Naturally, he faced resentment and prejudice – all successful people do, and those who are successful in politics more than most. Was William Wallace a politician? Of course he was. The entirety of his recorded life – other than Blind Harry's contribution – relates to political activity by a man of the political community who had, or more likely made, an opportunity to act in a sphere of government normally reserved for more elevated individuals. Most of William's political activity was of the military kind – he was a very violent man, one who enjoyed battle, as was the fashion of his class and time. Fortunately for Scottish historians, he was in the right place at the right time and applied his violent nature to the needs of his prince and his country just when they needed him most.

NOTES

1. WILLIAM WALLACE, KNIGHT OF SCOTLAND

1 John of Fordoun, Andrew of Wyntoun and Walter Bower all take pains to ensure the reader is aware that William Wallace was the son of a noble knight, a member of the aristocratic and political community of Scotland.

2 The term 'Scots' is used throughout this volume to indicate the form of northern Middle English spoken in southern and eastern Scotland in the thirteenth and fourteenth centuries.

3 The scarcity of Scottish state records from the thirteenth and fourteenth century is, obviously, a problem for Scottish medievalists. However, there are several sources which indicate the general practice of the king's chapel (chancery). See the introductions to *Regesta Regum Scottorum* (*RRS*), vols 5 and 6, *Exchequer Rolls of Scotland*, vol. I and the *Register of the Great Seal of Scotland*, vol. 1.

4 G. Donaldson, *Scottish Historical Documents* (Edinburgh 1970) pp.29–30.

2. OF NOBLE KIN: THE SOCIETY OF WILLIAM WALLACE

1 *The Wallace* was one of the first books to be printed in Scotland and one of the volumes most likely to be found in Scottish households in the eighteenth and nineteenth centuries. Robert Burns was particularly moved by Scotland's hero: 'Scots wha hae wi' Wallace bled ...'

2 See the *Register of the Great Seal of Scotland* (*RMS*) and the *Regesta Regum Scottorum* (*RRS*) volumes for the reigns of William the Lion and Robert I, for examples of the wide variety of burdens that could be attached to property tenure.

3 It has been widely assumed by historians that women did not play a significant part in medieval political communities. It is clear that women did not give military service – a political activity – in person, and much more likely than not that they did not give jury service either, but they were responsible for ensuring that the duties attached to any property they owned were properly discharged. Several historians have asserted that women were not required to give homage to their superior lords or to the king. The latter can be disproved by a brief examination of the *Calendar of Documents relating to Scotland* (*CDS*) where, in addition to records of several individual acts of homage, a sizeable proportion of the names entered on the Ragman Roll are female. *CDS*, vol. 2, pp.194-211.

4 See the introduction to *Regesta Regum Scottorum* (*RRS*), vol. 5.

5 Acts of the Parliaments of Scotland, vol. 1, p.404.

6 See Andrew Ayton, *Knights and their Warhorses*, for a detailed study of the English nobility at war in the fourteenth century.

7   R. Nicholson, *Scotland: The Later Middle Ages*, pp.48–54.

8   A.A.M. Duncan, *Barbour's Bruce*, pp.670–8.

9   A.A.M. Duncan, *Scotland. The making of the Kingdom*, pp.507–8.

10 At the time of writing there had not been, as yet, a scholarly monograph study of the Battle of Bannockburn since McKenzie's volume published in 1913, which is now extremely dated.

11 M. Powicke, *The Thirteenth Century*.

12 G.W.S. Barrow, 'Lothian in the Wars of Independence' in *Scotland and its Neighbours in the Middle Ages*.

13 See the introduction to *RRS*, vol. 5, Robert I.

14 *CDS*, vol. 2, no. 857.

15 For an examination of military obligation in Scotland prior to the Wars of Independence, see G.W.S. Barrow's essay 'The Army of Alexander III' in *Scotland in the Reign of Alexander III*, (ed.) N. Reid.

16 See introduction to *RRS*, vol. 5, Robert I.

17 The armies raised by Scottish kings for the campaigns that resulted in the battles of Bannockburn, Myton, Halidon Hill and Neville's Cross were not the normal practice of war, but rare events engendered by unusual circumstances.

18 A.A.M. Duncan, *Scotland. The Making of the Kingdom*, p.381.

19 Harold Booton, 'Burgesses and Landed Men in North East Scotland'. PhD thesis, Aberdeen University, 1987. Elizabeth Ewan, *Town Life in Fourteenth Century Scotland*.

20 See Mayhew and Gemmill, *The Changing Value of Money in Medieval Scotland*, for a detailed examination of the Scottish economy and money supply in the late Middle Ages.

21 R. Nicholson, *Scotland: The Later Middle Ages*, chapter 1 and A.A.M. Duncan, *Scotland. The Making of the Kingdom*, chapters 12, 18 and 19.

22 P. McNeill and H. MacQueen (eds), *Atlas of Scottish History to 1707*, pp.231–42.

23 I am indebted to Mr Alex Woolf of St Andrews University for his views on the relationship between feudal tenure and the deliberate fostering of markets in particular locations.

24 *STS* miscellany, vol. 11.

25 Several examples of these instructions can be found in *CDS*, vols 2 and 3 and in *Rotuli Scotiae*.

26 *CDS*, vol. 3, pp.327–41.

27 *CDS*, vol. 3, p.400.

3 THE ROOTS OF THE WAR

1 G. Donaldson, *Scottish Historical Documents*.

2 There were a number of kings in Europe who were the subjects of other kings: Savoy, Navarre and Sicily all fell into this category at different times.

3 *Regesta Regum Scottorum*, vol. 5, Robert I.

4 Although Caddonlea was considered the traditional mustering point for Scottish armies heading south, it had been some considerable time since a Scottish army had been raised at all.

5 See the Progress of Edward I, reprinted in this volume.

6 *Calendar of Documents Relating to Scotland* (CDS), vol. 2, pp.194–211.

7 Rev. Stevenson, *Documents Illustrative of the History of Scotland*.

8 C. Brown, 'We are Cummand of gentlemen'. PhD Thesis, St Andrews University, 2004, also *Knights of Scotland*, History Press.

9 *Camerar Scocie*, Accounts of the Chamberlain of Scotland.

10 *CDS*, vol. 2, no. 832 and many others.

11 G. Donaldson, *Scottish Historical Documents*.

4 FROM GANGSTER TO GOVERNOR

1 James MacKay, *Brave Heart* (Edinburgh and London, 1995).

2 *Calendar of Documents relating to Scotland*, vol.2, p.194 etc.

3 A.A.M. Duncan, *Scotland. The Making of the Kingdom*, chapters 13, 14, 15.

4 I am indebted to Mr Peter Armstrong for bringing this item to my attention and for sending me the relevant article from *The Herald* (formerly *The Glasgow Herald*).

5 Wallace had gathered an army of some thousands by the late summer of 1297; self-evidently, he was effective at recruiting.

6 According to the charges brought against William, he 'in contempt of the King, had cut the said sheriff's body in pieces'.

7 Blind Harry, *The Wallace*.

8 Details of the locations of his imprisonment and of the allowances he and his compatriots received as prisoners of war in castles throughout England and Wales can be found in great quantity in *CDS*, vol.2. Interestingly, prisoner of war allowances reflect social status in the same way as the pay structures of waged English sol-

diers of the time, though only a handful of Scottish men-at-arms received any form of pay and those who did were the recipients of salaries as knights of the king's household.

9 R. Nicholson, *Scotland: The Later Middle Ages* (Edinburgh, 1974), Chapter 1. For a detailed examination of the social, legal and financial structures of the later medieval town in Scotland, see Elizabeth Ewan, *Town Life in Fourteenth Century Scotland*.

10 The origins of this belief are obscure, being apparently quite well established by the middle of the twentieth century.

11 *Regesta Regum Scottorum*, vol. 5.

12 Barbour, *The Bruce*.

13 Maxwell's translation of *Scalacronica* was reprinted by Luath Publications in 2000, and a new scholarly edition by Dr A. King and Dr M. Prestwich is in preparation at the time of writing. As the observations of a professional career soldier, *Scalacronica* is a particularly significant account of the Scottish wars of the fourteenth century.

14 E.M. Barron, *The Scottish War of Independence*. Barron made a case that the study of the Wars of Independence had been almost completely focused on events and individuals in the south and east of the country. What he saw as 'Celtic' Scotland had borne the burden of the wars against the English, but their contribution had been ignored. Although he 'over-egged his pudding' – and was prone to distortions of fact about the geographic origin of specific lords – Barron did have something of a case.

15 For an introduction to the business of how armies and conflicts 'work' it would be difficult to suggest anything other than Michael Handel's *Masters of War, Classical Strategic Thought* (New York, 1992).

5 THE BATTLE OF STIRLING BRIDGE

1 For Edward I to attend to the problem in person might give the Balliol party a certain degree of credibility.
2 The thousands who, according to English chroniclers, died on the battlefield do not seem to have been noticed by anyone else.
3 Even if there had been a shortage of arms after the spring of 1296, there had been ample time to acquire replacements before the late summer of 1297.
4 The provisions made for the support of Sir Edward Hastang under Edward II and Sir John de Strivelin of East Swinneburne (Swinburne, Northumberland) by Edward illustrate this sort of arrangement. See Chris Brown, *Knights of Scotland*, for a detailed examination of military service tenure conditions in Scotland in the later thirteenth to mid-fourteenth centuries.
5 The Battle of Evesham.
6 This was the policy adopted successfully by Robert I against Edward I in the years after Bannockburn.
7 See 'The Resistible Rise of Edwardian Government' in Fiona Watson, *Under the Hammer* (East Lothian, 1998).
8 *Calendar of Documents Relating to Scotland (CDS)*, vol. 2, no. 1375.
9 Stevenson, *Documents Illustrative of Scottish History*, no. 453.
10 G. Cameron Stone, *Glossary of the Construction and Decoration of Armour*.
11 Maitland Club, *Documents Illustrative of William Wallace, His Life and Times*.
12 There was a '*galeator*' or 'helmet-maker' in Perth in the reign of William the Lion, but such specialists would be few and far between. Most of the armour worn by

most of the troops was leather- and/or fabric-based and could be produced at home.

13 The website www.deremilitari.org carries a synopsis of arms and armour prices from England from the 1290s to the late 1330s. Scottish prices are likely to have been similar or very slightly higher.

14 'Munition' equipment – arms and armour issued to the soldiers as opposed to arms purchased privately by the soldier.

15 *Scalacronica* (Maxwell).

16 One of these castles was Dirleton, a major modern fortress in 1296; the other two may have been Yester and Hailes.

6 FROM VICTORY TO IGNOMINY

1 C. MacNamee, *William Wallace's Invasion of England* (1990).

2 G. Donaldson, *Scottish Historical Documents* (Edinburgh 1970) pp.45–6.

3 Maitland Club, *Documents Illustrative of William Wallace, His Life and Times.*

4 *Calendar of Documents Relating to Scotland* (CDS), vol. 2, no. 1323.

5 Many of the military tenure obligations in north-eastern England and south-eastern Scotland had their origins in the earlier 'Thanage' and 'Drengage' tenures that pre-dated the 'feudal' arrangements introduced in the twelfth century. See A.A.M. Duncan, *Scotland. The Making of the Kingdom* (1975) pp.161 & 327 and chapter 15, *Fief and Service* for an examination of the origins and development of different military land tenures in Scotland.

6   There was something in the region of 200 Scots in English custody after the Dunbar campaign. Bain's *Calendar of Documents Relating to Scotland (CDS)*, vol. 2, is informative about the various arrangements made for their allowances, custody and accommodation, their ransoms and, increasingly after the summer of 1297, their exchange for men who had been taken prisoner by the Scots.

7   C. MacNamee, *William Wallace's Invasion of Scotland* (1990).

8   *Ibid.*

9   Stevenson, *Documents Illustrative of the History of Scotland* (London, 1879) p.237.

10 G.W.S. Barrow, 'The Army of Alexander III' in N. Reid (ed.) *Scotland in the reign of Alexander III* (Edinburgh, 1990).

11 R. Nicholson, *Scotland: The Later Middle Ages* (Edinburgh, 1974) p.56.

12 C. MacNamee, *William Wallace's Invasion of Scotland* (1990).

13 For a detailed examination of the English army of the Falkirk campaign see H. Gough, *Scotland in 1298: Documents Relating to the Campaign of King Edward I in that Year* (London, 1888).

14 M. Powicke, *The Thirteenth Century* (Oxford, 1953) p.689.

15 R. Nicholson, *Scotland: The Later Middle Ages* (Edinburgh, 1974).

16 *CDS* vol.2, no.1011.

17 G.W.S. Barrow, *Robert the Bruce and the Community of the Realm of Scotland* (London, 1965).

18 A. Young, *Robert the Bruce's Rivals: The Comyns, 1212–1314* (East Linton, 1997).

19 *Ibid.* Chapter 4, 'A Responsible Aristocratic Governing Community, *c.*1260–86'.

7 EXILE AND DEFIANCE

1 R. Nicholson, *Scotland: The Later Middle Ages* (Edinburgh, 1974) p.61.

2 Bruce and Comyn had assumed the Guardianship before the end of 1298. M. Penman, *The Scottish Civil War* (Stroud, 2002).

3 All land was held from the king, not owned outright as we would understand it. 'Heritage' lands were properties whose tenure passed indefeasibly from father to son – so long as all of the stipulations of the original grant were fulfilled.

4 *Calendar of Documents Relating to Scotland (CDS)*, vol. 2, no. 857.

5 Although Edward planned to build at least one modern stone castle – at Linlithgow – his financial situation meant that he had to settle for a timber 'peel' there and others at Selkirk and Lochmaben. Plans for a fourth peel at Dunfermline were apparently shelved when it became apparent that Edward could not find the money for labourers to dig the ditch that would provide the foundation for the rampart.

6 See Fiona Watson's *Under the Hammer* (East Linton, 1998) for a detailed examination of Edward I's Scottish administration, in particular the chapter 'The Resistible Rise of Edwardian Government'.

7 *CDS*, vol. 4, no.477.

8 Stevenson, *Documents Illustrative of Scottish History* (Edinburgh, 1879) nos. 131 and 132.

9   Stevenson, *Documents Illustrative of Scottish History*
    (Edinburgh, 1879) no. 633.
10 G.W.S. Barrow, *Robert the Bruce and the Community of
    the Realm of Scotland* (London, 1965) p.184, quoting
    Palgrave, *Documents and Records Illustrating the History
    of Scotland* (London, 1837). The instruction orders
    that 'Sir John Comyn, Sir Alexander Lindsay, Sir David
    Graham and Sir Simon Fraser shall exert themselves
    until twenty days after Christmas to capture Sir William
    Wallace and hand him over to the king, who will watch to
    see how each of them conducts himself so that he can do
    most favour to whoever shall capture Wallace, with regard
    to exile or legal claims or expiation of past misdeeds.'

8 BUT WHAT WAS IT ALL *FOR*?

1   Declarations of the clergy and, apparently, the nobility
    after the St Andrews Parliament of 1309 and of course
    the Declaration of Arbroath.
2   G.W.S. Barrow, *Robert the Bruce* (London, 1965)
    pp.252–4. A.A.M. Duncan, *Nation of the Scots and the
    Declaration of Arbroath* (London, 1970).
3   For an account of the rule of the Guardians see N. Reid,
    '*Kingless Kingdom*', SHR. 61, 1982.
4   G.W.S. Barrow, *Robert the Bruce and the Community
    of the Realm of Scotland*, pp.19–21, 23–4, 46–7 and
    also A. Young, *The Comyns – Robert the Bruce's Rivals
    1212–1314*. (East Lothian, 1998) pp.93–5.
5   The Guardianship of 1295 was a committee of twelve,
    'likened by contemporary English commentators to the
    Twelve Peers of France … in fact it was a return to the
    Guardianship of 1286.' Young, *The Comyns*, p.140.

6 For further discussion of the Community of the Realm as a political concept and in particular the medieval concept of national as opposed to personal liberty, see G.W.S. Barrow 'The Idea of Freedom in Late Medieval Scotland', *Innes Review*, vol. 30, 1980.

7 R. Nicholson, *Scotland: The Later Middle Ages* (Edinburgh, 1974) p.26.

8 G.W.S. Barrow, *Robert the Bruce* p.20.

9 The release of King John into papal custody was a major success for the Scots, but it did not procure his liberty.

10 Barrow, *Robert the Bruce* pp.134 & 168.

11 For further discussion see Barrow, *The Scottish Clergy and the War of Independence*, SHR 31 (1962).

12 F. Watson, *Under the Hammer* (East Lothian, 1998) p.45.

13 G.W.S. Barrow, *Robert the Bruce* p.117.

14 '... even though the lords themselves were present with the [English] King in body, at heart they were on the opposite side' – *Chronicle* of Walter of Guisborough, quoted in Nicholson, *Scotland: The Later Middle Ages* p.54. Although the term 'good lordship' is one we associate more with the fifteenth century than the fourteenth or the thirteenth, that does not mean that it's absence or presence was not of crucial significance to the relationship between lord and tenant.

15 Duncan, *Nation of the Scots,* and the Declaration of Arbroath.

16 This would have been a common experience among those landlords who sided with the Scottish administration but whose property lay in the occupied areas.

17 F. Watson, *Under the Hammer* p.30.

18 F. Watson, 'The Enigmatic Lion' in *Image and Identity* (Edinburgh, 1998).

19 G.W.S. Barrow, *Robert the Bruce* p.147.

20 A. Young, *The Comyns* pp.21, 28, 69.

21 G.W.S. Barrow, *Robert the Bruce* p.179.

22 That the Scots could hold a parliament as far south as Rutherglen is a good indication of their confidence and of the effectiveness of the English occupation.

23 G.W.S Barrow, *Robert the Bruce* p.128.

24 *Ibid* p.149.

25 A.A.M. Duncan examines the income of Scottish kings before the war in *Scotland, the Making of the Kingdom* (Edinburgh, 1975) pp.596–8.

26 F. Watson, *Under the Hammer* p.115.

27 *Ibid*, p.30.

28 *Ibid*, p.208.

29 C.J. Neville, 'Earls of Strathearn' SHR 65 1986.

30 A.A.M. Duncan, *Nation of the Scots*.

31 N. Reid, *Kingless Kingdom*.

32 The innovation was limited to the deployment. For an examination of military service obligations see Barrow, 'The Army of Alexander III's Scotland' in *Scotland in the Reign of Alexander III*, (ed.) N. Reid (Edinburgh, 1990).

33 It is difficult to see what more they could have hoped for.

34 Vague use of the words 'the right' in Robert Bruce's surrender pact suggest that Edward was prepared to consider using Bruce to keep John out of Scotland (F. Watson, *Under the Hammer*). Edward's confidence in Robert's dependability after the surrender of the Guardians has been questioned because of the requirement that he provide a keeper for Kildrummy Castle that 'he himself would be willing to answer for', but since Edward used the same phrase in an indenture with one of his own lords – Clifford – perhaps we should not read too much into it.

35 N. Reid, *Kingless Kingdom*.

9 DEATH AND IMMORTALITY

1 A larger property carried more of a burden (usually) than a smaller one, but not a different obligation.
2 Titles with the words 'holy', 'grail', 'Templar', 'mystery' and 'blood' often fall into this category.
3 Continental names abound in Scottish history: Fraser, Comyn, Lindsay, Sinclair and of course Bruce.
4 James McKay, *William Wallace: Braveheart* (Edinburgh, 1995) p.173.
5 G.W.S. Barrow, *Robert the Bruce* p.29.
6 A.A.M. Duncan, *Barbour's Bruce* (Edinburgh, 1997) introduction.
7 A.A.M. Duncan, *Scotland. The Making of the Kingdom* (Edinburgh, 1975) pp.378–91.
8 *Regesta Regum Scottorum*, introduction.
9 See Andrew Ayton, *Knights and their Warhorses* (Surrey, 1997).
10 G.W.S. Barrow, *Lothian in the Wars of Independence*.
11 C. Brown, Chapter 2, 'Lothian Families' in *Knights of Scotland*.
12 Antony Bek, Bishop of Durham, was entrusted with the recovery of three castles, Dirleton and two others, in the summer of 1298 before the Battle of Falkirk.
13 Fordoun, Wyntoun and Bower chronicles.

GLOSSARY

Advowson	right of appointment to a parish benefice
Aketon	a protective padded garment
Bailie	a sheriff's officer
Bondi	peasants
Carucate	a measure of land
Charger	a cavalry horse
Covered	armoured horses
Ferrand	a colour (of horses)
Haubergeon	protective padded garment
Hauberk	chainmail shirt
Hobelars	light cavalry or mounted infantry
Husbandmen	farm tenants
Jack	protective padded garment
Liard	a colour (of horses)
Librate	a measure of land
Magnates	the greater nobility
Marcate	a measure of land
Mark/merk	two-thirds of a pound; 13*s* 4*d*
Nativi	peasants

Oxgang	a measure of land
Restauro	compensation for warhorses lost on active service
Rustici	peasants
Servi	peasants
Sheriff	chief local officer of the Crown
Teinds	church taxation (tithes in England)
Verge	the household of the king of Scotland
Villein	peasant
Wappinschaw	a day for military training and weapons inspection
Wardrobe	the cash department of the households of English kings

SELECT BIBLIOGRAPHY

PRIMARY SOURCE MATERIAL

Acts of the Parliaments of Scotland. C. Innes (London, 1844)

Anglo-Scottish Relations, 1174–1328, Some Selected Documents. E.L.G. Stones (London, 1965)

Calendar of Close Rolls. (HMSO, London, 1892–1907)

Calendar of Documents Relating to Scotland. Vol. 5. G. Simpson and J. Galbraith (Edinburgh, 1988)

Calendar of Documents Relating to Scotland. Vols 1–4. J. Bain (Edinburgh, 1881–88)

Calendar of Inquisitions (Miscellaneous). (HMSO, London, 1916)

Calendar of Inquisitions Post Mortem. (HMSO, London, 1908–10)

Carte Monialium de Northberwic. (Bannatyne Club, Edinburgh, 1847)

Chronicles of the Reigns of Edward I and Edward II. Ed. W. Stubbs (London, 1882)

Chronicle of Holyrood. Ed. O. Anderson (SHS Edinburgh, 1938)

Chronicles (of Jean Froissart). Tr. & ed. G. Brereton (London, 1968)

Chronicon de Lanercost. (Bannatyne Club, Edinburgh, 1839)

Documents Illustrative of the History of Scotland. J. Stevenson (Edinburgh, 1870)

Edward I and the Throne of Scotland, 1290–96. E.L.G. Stones and G. Simpson (Oxford, 1978)

Exchequer Rolls of Scotland. Vol. 1. Ed. J. Stuart and G. Burnett (Edinburgh, 1876)

Liber Sancte Marie de Calchou. (Bannatyne Club, Edinburgh, 1846)

Liber Sancte Marie de Melros. (Bannatyne Club, Edinburgh, 1887)

Records of the Wardrobe and Household. Ed. F. and C. Byerley (HMSO, 1985)

Regesta Regum Scottorum. Vol. 5. Ed. A.A.M. Duncan (Edinburgh University Press, 1988)

Regesta Regum Scottorum. Vol. 6. Ed. B. Webster (Edinburgh University Press, 1982)

Registrum de Sancte Marie de Neubotle. Ed. C. Innes (Edinburgh, 1849)

Registrum Honoris de Morton. (Bannatyne Club, Edinburgh 1853)

Rotuli Scotiae. J. MacPherson (Record Commission, London, 1814–19)

Scalacronica of Sir Thomas Grey. Maxwell (1913)

Scotichronicon of Walter Bower. Ed. D. Watt (Aberdeen, 1991)

Scottish Historical Documents. G. Donaldson (Edinburgh, 1974)

Sourcebook of Scottish History. Ed. W. Croft Dickinson, G. Donaldson and I. Milne (Edinburgh, 1952)

The Bruce. J. Barbour. Ed. A.A.M. Duncan (Edinburgh, 1997)

The Chartulary of Coldstream. Ed. C. Rogers (London, 1879)

The Chronicle of Lanercost. Tr. H. Maxwell (Glasgow, 1913)

The Chronicle of Walter of Guisborough. Ed. H. Rothwell (Camden, 1957)

The Exchequer Rolls of Scotland, J. Stuart and G. Burnett (Edinburgh, 1978)

The Original Chronicle of Andrew of Wyntoun. Ed. J. Amours (Edinburgh, 1907)

The Register of the Great Seal of Scotland. Ed. J. Thomson (Edinburgh, 1912)

The Scottish King's Household. Ed. M. Bateson (SHS Miscellany, Edinburgh, 1904)

Vita Edwardus Secundus. Ed. N. Denholm-Young (London, 1957)

SECONDARY SOURCES AND SPECIALIST MATERIAL

A Distant Mirror. B. Tuchman (London, 1979)

A Historical Geography of Scotland. G. Whittington & I.G. White (eds) (London, 1983)

A History of England. Sir Charles Oman (London, 1910)

A History of Scotland. P.F. Tyler (Edinburgh, 1828–43)

A History of the Art of War. Sir Charles Oman (London, 1898)

A History of the Scottish People. T.C. Smout (Glasgow, 1969)

An Antidote to the English. N. Macdougall (East Lothian, 2001)

An Atlas of Scottish History to 1707. P. McNeill & H. MacQueen (Edinburgh, 1996)

Armies and Warfare in the Middle Ages. M. Prestwich (New Haven, 1996)

Aymer de Valence. J.R.S. Phillips (Oxford, 1972)

Bannockburn. J. Morris (Cambridge, 1914)

Border History of England and Scotland. P. Ridpath (Berwick, 1848)

Chivalry. M. Keen (London, 1984)

Civilisation and Capitalism. F. Braudel (London, 1981)

Conquest, Co-existence and Change: Wales 1063–1415. R. Davis (Oxford, 1987)

David II. M. Penman (East Lothian, 2002)

Early Travellers in Scotland. P. Hume Brown (Edinburgh, 1891)

Edward Bruce's Invasion of Ireland. O. Armstrong (London, 1923)

Edward I. M. Prestwich (London, 1988)

Edward I and Wales. T. Herbert & G. Jones (Cardiff, 1988)

Edward III and Chivalry. J. Vale (Woodbridge, 1982)

Edward III and the Scots. The Formative Years of a Military career. R. Nicholson (Oxford, 1965)

Essays on the Scottish Nobility. K. Stringer (Ed.) (Edinburgh, 1985)

European Armour 1066–1700. C. Blair (New York, 1972)

Europe in the Late Middle Ages. J. Hale (Ed.) (London, 1965)

Freedom and Authority. T. Brothers tone & D. Ditchburn (eds) (East Lothian, 2000)

Glossary of the Construction of Arms and Armour. G. Cameron Stone (London 1978)

History of Scotland. P. Hume Brown (Cambridge, 1911)

Hunting and Hunting Reserves in Medieval Scotland. J.M. Gilbert (Edinburgh, 1979)

Image and Identity. Broun & Lynch (eds) (Edinburgh, 1998)

Independence and Nationhood. A. Grant (London, 1984)

Kingship and Unity. G.W.S. Barrow (London, 1981)

Knights and Warhorses. A. Ayton (Woodbridge, 1994)

Land and Society in Early Scotland. R. A. Dodgson (Oxford, 1981)

Medieval Religious Houses in Scotland. E. Easson (London, 1957)

Military Obligation in England. M. Powicke (Connecticut, 1975)

New Light on Aberdeen. J. Smith (Ed.) (Aberdeen, 1985)

North-East England in the Middle Ages. R. Lomas (Edinburgh, 1992)

Numbers, Prediction and War. R. & T. Dupuy (New York, 1985)

RCAHMS Inventory of East Lothian. (HMSO, 1926)

RCAHMS Inventory of the City of Edinburgh. (HMSO, 1951)

RCAHMS, Midlothian and West Lothian. (HMSO, 1929)

Robert the Bruce. A Life Chronicled. C. Brown (Stroud, 2004)

Robert the Bruce and the Community of the Realm of Scotland. G.W.S. Barrow (London, 1965)

Robert the Bruce's Irish Wars. S. Duffy (Stroud, 2002)

Robert the Bruce's Rivals: The Comyns. A. Young (East Linton, 1997)

Scotland and England, 1286–1817. R. Mason (ed.) (Edinburgh, 1987)

Scotland and Europe. D. Ditchburn (East Lothian, 2001)

Scotland and its Neighbours in the Middle Ages.
G.W.S. Barrow (London, 1992)

Scotland and the Crusades. A. MacQuarrie (Edinburgh, 1997)

Scotland and the Low Countries. G. Simpson (ed.) (East Linton, 1996)

Scotland and War. N. Macdougall (ed.) (Edinburgh, 1991)

Scotland: a New History. M. Lynch (London, 1991)

Scotland from the Earliest Times to 1603. W. Croft Dickinson (Oxford, 1977)

Scotland in the Reign of Alexander III. N. Reid (ed.) (Edinburgh, 1990)

Scotland's Black Death. K. Jillings (Stroud, 2004)

Scotland's Relations with England. A Survey to 1701. W. Ferguson (Edinburgh, 1977)

Scotland: The Later Middle Ages. R. Nicholson (Edinburgh, 1974)

Scotland, the Making of the Kingdom. A.A.M. Duncan (Edinburgh, 1975)

Scottish Handwriting. G. Simpson (ed.) (Aberdeen, 1977)

Scottish Heraldic Seals. J. Stevenson & M. Wood (Glasgow, 1940)

Studies in the Agrarian History of England in the Thirteenth Century. E. Kosminsky (Oxford, 1956)

The Anglo-Norman Era in Scottish History.
G.W.S. Barrow (Oxford, 1980)

The Art of War in Western Civilization. A. Jones (Chicago, 1987)

The Battle of Bannockburn. W.M. McKenzie (Glasgow, 1913)

The Battle of Neville's Cross. D. Rollason & M. Prestwich (eds) (Stamford, 1998)

The Black Douglases. M. Brown (East Linton, 1998)

The Black Prince's Expedition 1355–57. H. Hewitt (Manchester, 1958)

The Changing Value of Money in Medieval Scotland. N. Mayhew & E. Gemmill (Cambridge, 1996)

The Edwards in Scotland 1296–1377. J. Bain (Edinburgh, 1901)

The English Wool Trade in the Middle Ages. T. Lloyd (Cambridge, 1977)

The Exercise of Power in Medieval Scotland. S. Boardman & A. Ross (eds) (Chippenham, 2003)

The Fourteenth Century. M. McKisack (Oxford, 1959)

The Hundred Years War. C. Allmand (Cambridge, 1998)

The Hundred Years War. J. Sumption (London, 1990)

The Kingdom of the Scots. G.W.S. Barrow (London, 1973)

The Knight in Medieval England. P. Coss (Stroud, 1993)

The Knights of Edward I. C. Moor (Harleian Society, 1930)

The Longbow, a Social History. R. Hardy (London, 1992)

The Low Countries and the Hundred Years War. H. Lucas (Michigan, 1929)

The Maxtones of Cultoqhuey. A. Maxtone (Perth, 1936).

The Medieval Church in Scotland. J. Dowden (Glasgow, 1910)

The Medieval Warhorse. R. Davis (London, 1989)

The New Towns of the Middle Ages. M. Beresford (London, 1957)

The Nobility of Later Medieval England. K.B. Macfarlane (Oxford, 1973)

The Normans in Scotland. R. Ritchie (Edinburgh, 1954)

The Parliaments of Scotland. R. Rait (Glasgow, 1924)

The Rose and the Thistle. S. Mapstone & J. Wood (eds) (East Lothian, 1998)

The Scots Peerage. Sir J. Balfour Paul (Edinburgh, 1904–14)

The Scottish Castle. S. Cruden (Edinburgh, 1981)

The Scottish Civil War. M. Penman (Stroud, 2003)

The Scottish War of Independence. E.M. Barron (Inverness, 1934)

The Scottish War of Independence. W. Burns (1874)

The Second Scottish War of Independence. C. Brown (Stroud, 2002)

The Social and Economic Development of Scotland before 1603. I.F. Grant (Edinburgh, 1930)

The Surnames of Scotland. G. Black (Edinburgh, 1999)

The Thirteenth Century. F. Powicke (Oxford, 1953)

The Three Edwards; War and State in England, 1272–1377. M. Prestwich (London, 1980)

The Ties that Bound: Peasant Families in Medieval England. B. Hanawalt (Oxford, 1986)

The Tournament in England, 1100–1400. J. Barker (Stroud, 1986)

The Tyranny and Fall of Edward II, 1321–26. N. Fryde (Cambridge, 1979)

The Wars of the Bruces. C. MacNamee (East Linton, 1997)

The Welsh Wars of Edward I. J. Morris (London, 1901)

Town life in Fourteenth Century Scotland. E. Ewan (Edinburgh, 1990)

Understanding Defeat. T. Dupuy (New York, 1990)

Under the Hammer. F. Watson (East Linton, 1998)

War and Government in the Middle Ages. J. Gillingham & J. Holt (eds) (Woodbridge, 1984)

War in Medieval Society. J. Barrie (London, 1974)

War in the Middle Ages. P. Contamine (Oxford, 1986)

Warrior Race. L. James (London, 2001)

William Wallace. A. Fisher (Edinburgh, 1986)

UNPUBLISHED THESES AND PAPERS

The Kingship of David II. Michael Penman (St Andrews University, 1998)

Burgesses and Landed Men in North-east Scotland in the Later Middle Ages. Harold Booton (Aberdeen University, 1987)

Military Service of Northumbrian Knights. A. King (Durham University Medieval Conference, 2001)

Technology and Military Technology in Medieval England. Randall Storey (University of Reading, 2003)

A Lyon in the Field, Continuity and Change in Scottish Warfare 1057–1460. C.A. Brown (BCLA, Galashiels, 1985)

ARTICLES

'The Development of Scottish Border Lordship, 1332–58.' M. Brown, *Historical Research*. Vol. 75, no. 171 (February 1997)

'A Late Fourteenth-Century Coin Hoard from Tranent.' J. Bateson & P. Stott, *Proceedings of the Society of Antiquaries of Scotland*. 120 (1990)

'Archaeological Excavations at Cockpen Medieval Parish Church, Midlothian, 1993.' O'Sullivan, *Proceedings of the Society of Antiquaries of Scotland*. 125 (1995)

'Chronicle Propaganda in Fourteenth Century Scotland.' S.Boardman, *Scottish Historical Review* 76 (1977)

'Edinburgh Castle, Iron Age fort to Garrison Fortress.' P. Yeoman, *Fortress Magazine* 4 (1990)

'Excavations at Springwood Park, Kelso.' P. Dixon, *Proceedings of the Society of Antiquaries of Scotland*.

'Excavations South of Bernard Street., Leith, 1980.' N. Holmes, *Proceedings of the Society of Antiquaries of Scotland*. 115 *f*. (1985)

'In the Territory of Auchencrow: Long Continuity or Late Development in early Scottish Field Systems.' J. Donnelly, *Proceedings of the Society of Antiquaries of Scotland*. 130 (2000)

'Lothian in the First War of Independence.' G.W.S. Barrow, *Scottish Historical Review* 55 (1976)

'New Light on Old Coin Hoards from the Aberdeen Area.' D. Evans & S. Thain, *Proceedings of the Society of Antiquaries of Scotland*. 119 (1989)

'North Berwick, East Lothian; its Archaeology Revisited.' D. Hall & D. Bowler, *Proceedings of the Society of Antiquaries of Scotland*. 127 (1997)

'Scottish Arms in the Bellenville Roll.' C. Campbell, *Scot. Geneal*, 25

'Sprouston, Roxburghshire.' I. Smith, *Proceedings of the Society of Antiquaries of Scotland*. 121 (1991)

'The Aftermath of War.' G.W.S. Barrow, *Transactions of the Royal Historical Society*. Fifth Series, 28 (1978)

'The Lunan Valley Project: Medieval Rural Settlement in Angus.' D. Pollock, *Proceedings of the Society of Antiquaries of Scotland*. 115 (1985)

'The Sigillography of the Ragman Roll.' B. McAndrew, *Proceedings of the Society of Antiquaries of Scotland*. 129 (1999)

'The Use of Money in Scotland, 1124–1230.' W. Scott, *SHR* 58 (1979)

'The War of the Scots, 1306–23', Prothero Lecture, *TRHS* (1992)

'Thomas of Coldingham.' J. Donnelly, *SHR* 59 (1980)

'War, Allegiance and Community in the Anglo-Scottish Marches: Teviotdale in the Fourteenth Century.' Dr M. Brown, *Northern History*, 41 (2004)

INDEX

If you enjoyed this book, you may also be interested in…

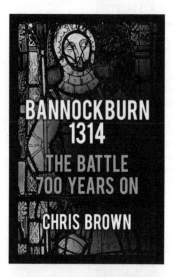

Bannockburn 1314

CHRIS BROWN

The Battle of Bannockburn is the most celebrated battle in history between Scotland and England. Chris Brown's startling account recreates the campaign and battle from the perspectives of both the Scots and the English. Only now, through an in-depth investigation of the contemporary narrative sources as well as the administrative records, and through a new look at the terrain where the battle was fought, can we come to firmer conclusions on what exactly happened and why.

978 0 7509 5379 5

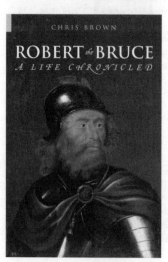

Robert the Bruce

CHRIS BROWN

Much is known about Robert the Bruce's military campaigns for Scottish Independence in Scotland and England but what about his expeditions to Ireland? In 1315 a fleet-load of Scots Bannockburn veterans put ashore at what is now County Antrim. The Anglo-Scottish conflict had transferred itself to Irish soil and it amounted to a full scale invasion. What the Bruce brothers hoped to achieve from their Irish venture is hotly debated. This lavishly illustrated study attempts to answer the questions about this and tells the story of the invasion itself and the battles that followed.

978 0 7524 2575 7

Visit our website and discover thousands of
other History Press books.

www.thehistorypress.co.uk